# A Description Of Ventilators: Whereby Great Quantities Of Fresh Air May With Ease Be Conveyed Into Mines, Goals, Hospitals, ... By Stephen Hales ......

Stephen Hales

**Nabu Public Domain Reprints:**

You are holding a reproduction of an original work published before 1923 that is in the public domain in the United States of America, and possibly other countries. You may freely copy and distribute this work as no entity (individual or corporate) has a copyright on the body of the work. This book may contain prior copyright references, and library stamps (as most of these works were scanned from library copies). These have been scanned and retained as part of the historical artifact.

This book may have occasional imperfections such as missing or blurred pages, poor pictures, errant marks, etc. that were either part of the original artifact, or were introduced by the scanning process. We believe this work is culturally important, and despite the imperfections, have elected to bring it back into print as part of our continuing commitment to the preservation of printed works worldwide. We appreciate your understanding of the imperfections in the preservation process, and hope you enjoy this valuable book.

principally intended for the Service of Sea farers; and as your Lordſhips were pleaſed to encourage and promote the Thing, by ordering a Trial to be made thereof: ſo I thought it not improper, to addreſs myſelf on this occaſion to your Lordſhips, who have the Super-intendency of the Royal Navy.

THERE is no doubt but it will fully anſwer your Lordſhips tender Care and Concern for the Welfare of Navigators, as it will contribute much to their Health, by ſupplying them, in exchange for a very noxious, with Plenty of freſh Air, that genuine Cordial of Life: For that wonderful Fluid the Air, which, by infinite Combinations with natural Bodies, produces ſurprizing Effects,

as

# DEDICATION.

as it is on the one Hand when pure, the chief Nourisher and Preserver of the Life of Animals and Vegetables; so, when foul and putrid, it is the great Principle of their Destruction.

As Sea-farers, that Valuable and Useful Part of Mankind, have many Hardships and Difficulties to contend with, so it is of great Importance to obviate as many of them as possible: And as the noxious Air in Ships has hitherto been one of their greatest Grievances, by making sick and destroying multitudes of them; so the finding a Means to prevent this great Evil, is of vastly more Consequence to Navigation, than the Discovery of the Longitude; as being a Means of saving innumerable more Lives, than that would do. And therefore it was what well deserved the most diligent Researches; and even the trying, every the lowest Degree of Probability of effecting it.

When it is found, that Men can, with greater Safety to their Lives, traverse the vast Expanse of Waters, it will be a great Advantage to Navigation, and Traffick will thereby be much inlarged.

That your Lordships have not herein been countenancing a vain fruitless Attempt, is evident, not only from considering the Effects of the Engine, which exchanges great Quantities of bad, for good Air; but also from the Event, it having been found
very

very salutary by the *Swedes*, who have made the Trial.

'Tis a good Symptom that we are got upon a right Scent, when it leads not only to the Thing first sought for; but also to many other useful Discoveries, as we see this does.

We have here an Instance, that the Study of Natural Philosophy is not a meer trifling Amusement, as some are apt to imagine: For it not only delights the Mind, and gives it the most agreeable Entertainment, in seeing in every thing the Wisdom of the great Architect of Nature: But it is also the most likely Means, to make the Gift of kind Providence, this natural World, the more beneficial

ficial to us, by teaching us how, both to avoid what is Hurtful, and to pursue what is most Useful and Beneficial to us.

*I am,*

*With all due Respect,*

My Lords,

*Your Lordships*

*Obedient Humble Servant,*

*Stephen Hales.*

# THE PREFACE.

*IT may not be improper to give an Account how I, who am neither concerned nor skilled in naval Affairs, came first to think of these Ventilators*; viz. *In the beginning of September in the Year* 1740, *I wrote to Dr.* Martin *Physician to Lord* Cathcart, *General of the Forces which lay imbarked at* Spithead, *for an Expedition in* America, *to propose (besides the usual sprinkling between Decks with Vinegar) the hanging up very many Cloths dipped in Vinegar, in proper Places between Decks, in order*

*to*

*to make the Air more wholesome: And in case an infectious Distemper should be in any Ship, to cure the Infection with the Fumes of burning Brimstone.*

*It was from these Considerations, which often recurred to my Thoughts, that it occurred to me the March following, that large Ventilators would be very serviceable, in making the Air in Ships more wholesome; this I was so fully satisfied of, that I immediately drew up an Account of it; several Copies of which were communicated, both by my self and others, to many Persons of Distinction, and Members of the* Royal Society: *Before whom I laid a large Account of it, which was read in their Presence the* May *following, as appears by the Minutes of the Society.*

# PREFACE.

November *the fixth following,* viz. *in the Year* 1741, Martin Triewald, *Captain of* Mechanicks *and Military Architect to the King of* Sweden, *and Fellow of the* Royal Society *at* London, *in a Letter to* Cromwell Mortimer *M. D. and Secretary of the* Royal Society, *fays, that* "this Spring he had invented a Machine, for the Ufe of his Majefty's Men of War, which went to block up Petersburgh, in order to draw out the bad Air from under their Decks, the leaft of which does exhauft 36172 cubick Feet of Air in an Hour," *that is at the Rate of* 21732 *Tuns in twenty four Hours.*

*It were a very extraordinary Circumftance, that two Perfons at fo great a Diftance from each other, without getting a Hint of it, one from the*

*the other, should happen to hit on inventing a like very useful Engine.*

*And in his Letter to Dr.* Mortimer, *dated the 8th of June* 1742, *he says,* " *that he wrote a Deduction of the Usefulness of his Engine on board Ships only, which has been printed by Order of His Majesty, and been distributed among the Officers of the Navy.*"

*For this Engine he had a Privilege for Life granted him by the King and Senate of* Sweden, *dated the* 20th October 1741, *which Privilege is printed at the end of the above mentioned Deduction.*

*A Translation of which ingenious Treatise, was communicated to me by Dr.* Mortimer; *in which he says,* " *In Hospitals and Barracks for the Sick, this Machine is placed in the Garret, from whence two or three*
" *Pipes*

"  *Pipes go down, some Inches thro'*
"  *the Ceiling, into each Room where*
"  *the Sick lie; and thus draw out all*
"  *the unwholesome Air and Stench,*
"  *which does more harm than any*
"  *Physick can repair. And at the*
"  *same time, has this accidental Be-*
"  *nefit, That those who begin to mend,*
"  *may give themselves a proper Ex-*
"  *ercise, in working the Machine:*
"  *Only they ought to take care to keep*
"  *all the Garret-Windows open,*
"  *while the Machine is a going. In*
"  *Men of War and Hospital-Ships,*
"  *this Machine is placed on the up-*
"  *per Deck, directly over the great*
"  *or any other Hatch: And then the*
"  *Pipe, which goes down between the*
"  *Decks, draws out the unwholesome*
"  *Air; which is instantly supplied*
"  *by fresh."*

*This*

*This Treatise, he says, was read before the* Royal Academy of Sweden *the third day of* April 1742. " *which noble Work the Academy wish to see soon printed.*" *This was eleven Months after mine was laid before the* Royal Society.

*And in his Letter to Baron* Wasenberg, *Envoy from the King of* Sweden, *dated the* 22d *of* April 1743, *which the Baron did me the Favour of communicating to me, he says,* " *that every* Swedish *Man of War, and Hospital-Ship, was last Year furnished with one of my Engines; which had not been done, in case they had not experienced the Benefit of the same, the Campaign before that.*" *So that a Trial was made with these Ventilators in the Year* 1741, *which proved a very sickly Summer in the* Swedish *Fleet, except*

# PREFACE.

*except only in the Ship or Ships, which were refreshed by Ventilators: A strong Instance of their great Usefulness; which induced the* Swedes *to put them into every Man of War and Hospital-Ship, the Year following.*

*And Mr.* Triewald *further says, that in the Summer of the Year* 1742, *he had sent one of his Engines, calculated for a Sixty Gun Man of War, to* France; *which being approved of by the* Royal Academy of Sciences *at* Paris, *the King of* France *has ordered all the Men of War to be furnished with the like Ventilators.*

*Being informed, while this Book was printing, that it was said that* Nathaniel Henshaw M. D. F. R. S. *had long since made a like Proposal, for sweetning the Air of Ships, in a Treatise called* Aëro-Chalinos, *or a* Register *for the Air, printed in the Year*

*Year* 1677; *having never seen the Book, I sent for it from the* Royal Society *Library.*

*In which Book is the following Proposal, viz. In order to have the Benefit of Change of Air, to another Country or Climate, almost at any Season, and that without going out of the House; he would have a Room, which he calls an Air-Chamber, to be built about twelve Feet square, and Air-tight every where; with a very large Pair of Organ-Bellows to be placed in the Room; to or from which, Air is to be conveyed through the Wall, by a Copper Pipe; with Valves to open inward or outward, as Occasion shall require. With these Bellows, the Air in the Room is either to be condensed and made heavier, by forcing Air in, or lighter, by conveying Air out of the Room.*

*Now,*

# PREFACE. xvii

*Now, supposing when the Air is so light, as to have the Quicksilver in the Weather-Glass fallen to its lowest Mark twenty eight Inches, that a Person should then desire to be in an Air so heavy, as to raise the Mercury three Inches higher up to settled fair; then the Air must be forcibly drove into the Room by the Bellows; and* vice versa *it must be drawn out, when it is required to have the Air in the Room so much lighter than the outward Air.*

*But in both these Cases, the Force of the inclosed Air to push out in a condensed state, or of the outward Air to press into the Room, in a rarefied state, would be no less than 38304 Pounds Troy, supposing the Room to be twelve Feet square every way. And the Force of the Air against the Glass of the Window, supposing it to be a*

Foot

*Foot square, would be* 266 *Pounds. And the Pressure of Air on the Bellows, if they were two Feet broad and six Feet long, would be equal to* 3192 *Pounds: for in all these Cases, the Pressure would be equal to a Quantity of Mercury three Inches deep, and as broad as the sides of the Room, or surface of the Bellows.*

*He proposes by this means to cure intermitting Fevers, by having the Air in the Room rarefied in the cold Fit, and condensed in the hot Fit; during the whole time of which, the Patient is to continue therein: And recommends the use of it, among other Distempers, to cure the Stone and the Pox.*

*He proposes also to prevent Sea-Sickness thereby, by having a Man thus shut up in a close Cabin in a compressed Air: This, I suppose, has led some to say, that this and my Proposal*

*sal* are the *same*. But how wide is their Difference! My Ventilators are intended to promote a free Perspiration and Breathing, by conveying great Quantities of fresh Air into Ships, in exchange for very bad Air. On the contrary, Dr. Henshaw's Contrivance would make a good Air, by confining it, very bad, and thereby retard Perspiration, and incommode the Breathing, and so cause, instead of preventing, Sickness: And were his of any real Benefit, it could only be so to very few, and that by turns; whereas mine will be beneficial to the whole Ship's Crew at the same time. Besides, the Make of my Ventilators is very different from that of Organ-Bellows.

I should not have troubled the World with the Recital of this foolish Proposal, had it not been to obviate a false Report, which might have prevailed

*vailed much more, especially considering that the Book itself, which refutes it, is now grown scarce.*

*As these Ventilators are like to prove of great Benefit to Mankind, in many other Respects than are here mentioned, or can as yet be thought of; so it will be of great use, if those who shall have made farther Improvements, will, from time to time, communicate them; as also an Account of the Difficulties or Success they have met with in putting the Things here proposed in execution.*

---

ERRATA.

PAGE 5. penult. for Z. r. N. p. 13. l. 14. r. 526. p. 17. l. 10. for *Pumps* r. *Damps*. p. 50. l. 2. for *when* r. *where*. p. 54. l. 24. for *Holds* r. *Folds*. p. 66. l. 9. r. C. B. p. 73. l 8. r. *same Manner.* p. 141. l. 14 r *deducting*.

# A
# DESCRIPTION
## OF
## VENTILATORS, &c.

### ( I. )

1. BEING informed, how very Offensive the close confined Air in Ships was, and that chiefly where there were a great number of Men, as in Men of War, and especially, in Transport and Hospital Ships; it occurred to me, that this Inconvenience might, in a great Measure, be obviated by means of large Bellows, either such as are made for Organs, which move on a Joint on one end, or else are made square or round, like what are called lantern Bellows, which are raised and compressed on all sides,

being Cubes or Cylinders, capable of being lengthened or compressed. The first Sort seems to be the most commodious for these Purposes; but they may be made of any shape, as shall be found best to suit the Place where they are to be fixed.

2. AND whereas Smiths Bellows and Organ Bellows are heaved with Labour, because in them it is necessary to have the Air much compressed, that it might pass with Velocity and Force through small Orifices, it is proposed therefore to have the Valves and Passages through these Bellows very large, on which account they will be worked to and fro, with the greatest Ease imaginable, as is evident in the case of common Bellows, which will move up and down, with surprizing Ease, if their Valve be held open with a Finger. And the Case would be just the same, if the Bellows were very large, provided the Valves were proportionably large, and are also made to open and shut easily. For in this Case we only want to move a quantity of light uncompressed Air, from the outside to the inside of the Place where it is desired, or from within outward.
And

And since a Tun or forty Cubick Feet of Air in bulk, weighs but 300 Grains, which is not three quarters of an Ounce; suppose a Pair of Bellows were so large, as to contain a Tun, yet that Tun of Air would give little resistance to the contracting Bellows, provided the Valves and Wind-Pipes leading to and from them, were proportionably large: And for the same Reason, the Dilatation of the Bellows would be equally easy. Thus we breathe to and fro through a large Wind-Pipe, about sixteen Tuns of Air in twenty-four Hours, with little or no Labour. And in this consists the peculiar Excellence of this Contrivance; this Method of conveying Air being most simple, and analogous to the way which Nature makes use of, to convey fresh Air into the Lungs of Men, and of many other Animals, *viz.* by the easy rising and falling of the Midriff.

3. Now in order to make trial of the Method here proposed, I caused two Pair of Bellows to be made in the following manner, *viz.* being accommodated with a Grainery, by the Favour of Governour *George Pit* Esq; at the House of *Anthony Duncombe* Esq;

which was thirty Feet long, and contained about two hundred Tuns of Air; in the lesser adjoining Room, were placed, side by side, two large Boxes, which were ten Feet long, five Feet wide, and two Feet deep, in the clear within side. *Fig.* 1. A B C D, describes one of the Boxes, in the middle of which was fixed a broad Partition or Midriff, which was made to move up and down from A to C, on the Hinges X, by means of the Iron Rod Z R, which was fixed to the Midriff at Z, and passed through a small Hole in the Cover of the Box up to R; the like Partition, or Midriff, was in the other Box, with its Iron Rod Z R; which two Rods were fixed to a Lever or Arm F, G, *Fig.* 2. which moved on the fixed Centre O: So that by the alternate raising and pressing down of the Lever F, G, the Midriffs were also alternately raised and depressed, whereby these double Bellows were, at the same time, both drawing in Air and pouring it out; one of each Pair of Bellows, being in a dilating state, drew in the Air; while the other two, which were at the same time in a compressing state, blew it out. And that the Midriffs might be the lighter, they were made

made of four Bars or Rails length-wise, and as many across them breadth-wise, which were each three Inches broad and an Inch and quarter thick, swelling in the middle to give them Strength. The vacant Spaces were filled up with thin Pannels of Fir Board, like Wainscot Work.

4. THE Midriff Z X moving to and fro with its Edges very near, *viz.* $\frac{1}{20}$th of an Inch from the sides of the Box A, B, C, D, F, E, *Fig.* 1. very little Air, in comparison of the whole, will escape by the Edges; so that there will be no need of leathern sides, as in common Bellows: which Leather would not only be more expensive, but would also cause them to move much more heavily. And, that the Midriffs may move to and fro with the greater Ease, and without touching the sides of the Boxes, there is an Iron-Regulator fixed upright, *Fig.* 1. to the middle of the end of the Box A C from N to L; which being half an Inch thick, and an Inch broad, a Notch of the same depth is cut into the middle of the End of the Midriff at 𝔏, so that the Midriffs in rising and falling, suffer no other Bearing or Friction than what

is made between the *Regulator* and the Notch.

5. The end of the Box at A C must be made a little circular, that it may be the better adapted in all Parts, between A and C to the rising and falling Midriff; and if the Boards at this end of the Box be but half an Inch thick, such thin Boards will, on being nailed on, the more easily comply with, and be forced into the circular Shape of, the Ends of the Side-Boards to which they are nailed. And that these Boards might the better retain their circular Shape, circular Battings were nailed on their outside: But in the Ventilators on shipboard, for the sake of greater Strength, this circular Form was cut out of a thick Fir-Plank. At the other end X of the Midriff a slip of Leather may be nailed over the Joint at the Hinges, if needful. The Hinges were made of two pieces of Iron, one of which grasped the End of the Midriff at the side, the other was a flat piece of Iron six Inches long, one and a half broad, and half Inch thick, which was let into the Side-Board of the Ventilators; these two Irons were riveted together with a Rivet half Inch thick, which was the moving Joint. 6. All

6. All the Boards of which the Boxes are compoſed ought to have their Joints well ſecured with *Grooves* and *Tongues*, and have brown Paper paſted over them; and eſpecially near both the Ends they may be faſtned with Wood-Screws, to draw out, in order to rectify any thing that may be amiſs there.

7. The eight large Valves for the Air to paſs through were placed at the Hinge-End of the Boxes B K, *Fig.* 2. 1, 2, 3, 4, 5, 6, 7, 8. The Valve, Numb. 1. opens inward to admit the Air to enter, when the Midriff is depreſſed at the other End, by means of the Lever F G. And at the ſame time the Valve 3, in the lower Ventilator, is ſhut by the compreſſed Air which paſſes out at the Valve 4. But when that Midriff is raiſed, then the Valve 1 ſhuts, and the Air paſſes out at the Valve 2. And it is the ſame with the Valves 5, 6, 7, 8, of the other Box; ſo that when by the Motion of the Lever F G, the Midriffs are alternately riſing and falling, then two of the Ventilators are conſtantly drawing in Air, and two of them

at the same time are blowing it out at their proper Valves; the Air entering at the Valves 1, 3, 6, 8, and passing out at the Valves 2, 4, 5, 7.

8. THERE was fixed to the Ventilators before the Valves 2, 4, 5, 7, a Box Q, Q, N, M, *Fig.* 3. as a common Receptacle for all the Air which came out of those Valves; which Air passed off thro' the Trunk P, which was a Foot square in the Clear within; this Trunk passed thro' the Partition-Wall of the two Rooms. The Valves were hung on Leathern Hinges, which were fixed to their upper Side, which is best, because that Position will cause them always to shut of themselves by their own Weight. In Ships these Hinges ought to be made of Brass or Copper, to prevent rusting.

9. I MADE the Openings of the Valves at first, twelve Inches long and six wide, which was one hundredth part of the Breadth of each Midriff, they being fifty square Feet broad; but on trial, I found these Openings too narrow for the great Quantity of Air which was to pass thro' them.

them. I then made the Openings two Feet long, and seven Inches wide; which I found to be a sufficient degree of wideness, that being nearly $\frac{1}{44}$th part of the Breadth of each Midriff: which were moved up and down easily enough, notwithstanding each of them weighed on the Lever at RR, *Fig.* 2. thirty Pounds; which very little increased the Force requisite to move the Lever, because they counter-balanced each other's Weight: on which account two Pair of these Bellows, in this horizontal Posture, may be worked with more ease than one Pair.

10. IT is very requisite to make the Valves as light as possible; for when they weighed two Pounds, being made of red Fir half Inch thick, they did not open wide enough for the Air to pass freely. But when they were made about $\frac{1}{4}$th Inch thick, and of lighter white Fir, weighing but fifteen Ounces; being then raised, by the rushing Air, to an Opening of about forty-five Degrees, or half open; then the Midriffs were worked to and fro with ease enough. But to prevent the warping of these thin Valves, it was needful to let in, tack and glew on

them

them, Pieces or Fillets across each of them, *viz.* one at each End, and one in the Middle. It will contribute much to their Lightness, to have the lower more moveable part of the Valves much thinner than the upper part; which will require a thicker Substance of half an Inch, to nail the Hinges fast on; which, if made of Horses Hides, will be very tough and durable.

11. IF it were needful to make the Valves open wider, with more ease, it might be done by placing a Counter-balancing Weight, so as to make them shut with only one fourth Part of their Weight, or less, as I have found on Trial may be done: but there seems no need to make them go so very easy; tho' the Resistance that there is, is principally from the Valves: for when they are all set open, the Midriffs are moved up and down with much more Ease.

12. WHEN the Box QQ, with its Trunk P, was put over the Valves 2, 4, 5, 7. *Fig.* 2, and 3. so as to receive the Air which rushed out of them; then the Midriffs required a sensibly greater Force to move

them

them up and down: which shows that the Trunk P was not wide enough, notwithstanding it was a Foot square in the Clear within side. Whence I found, that the working of the Bellows, faster than at the Rate of sixty Strokes in a Minute, did not proportionably increase the Quantity of Air that was conveyed out of them: for when they worked at the Rate of eighty Strokes in a Minute, the Air not being able to pass off so fast at the Nose, was much compressed in the Bellows; which Air dilating again as the Bellows dilated, so much the less Air was sucked in at each Dilatation of the Bellows, and consequently so much the less passed off. Which is a Thing well worth the taking notice of, else there may be much superfluous Labour, when the Bellows are worked too fast, for the Air to pass as freely and fast off: for when the Bellows are large, they will convey great Quantities of Air, without being worked very fast, which will much lessen the Labour of working them.

( II. )

( II. )

13. IT is easy to make an Estimate of the great Quantities of Air, that are conveyed by these Bellows: For suppose the Midriffs rise and fall one Foot at each Stroke, which is enough, and that sixty Times in a Minute, that will amount to seventy-five Tuns in a Minute, and four Thousand five Hundred in an Hour; which will amount to one Hundred eight Thousand Tuns in twenty-four Hours. And the Trunk P being a Foot square, the Velocity of the Air, as it passes out thence, will be at the rate of three Thousand Feet in a Minute; which is at the rate of thirty-four Miles in an Hour. This, supposing no Air escaped between the Edges of the rising and falling Midriffs, and the Sides of the Boxes, for which, an Allowance is to be made; for which, supposing eight Miles are deducted, a large Allowance; That will be nearly the Velocity with which a Race-Horse goes, who runs four Miles in nine Minutes, which is at the rate of 26.6 Miles in an Hour. And more than

thrice

thrice the Velocity with which Fans impel Air, in winnowing Corn, when they are turned at the Rate of seventy Revolutions in a Minute.

14. Monsieur Mariotte found that a pretty strong Wind moves twenty-four Feet in a Second of Time, which is at the Rate of one Thousand four Hundred and Forty in a Minute; that is, at the Rate of Twelve and a half Miles in an Hour: which is about half the Velocity, with which the Wind rushes out of these Ventilators.

15. In my *Statical Essays*, Vol. II. pag. 326. it was found that the Air rushed out of a Pair of Smith's Bellows, at the Rate of 68.73 Feet in a Second of Time; that is, at the Rate of Seventy-eight Miles in an Hour, when compressed with a Force equal to the Weight of one Inch perpendicular Depth of Mercury, laying on the whole upper Surface of the Bellows.

16. But there is another Way whereby to estimate the Velocity, with which impelled

pelled Air passes out at any Orifice: this I tried by hanging a light Valve, which was six Inches long, and three and a half broad, over the Nose of the Bellows, by pliant Leathern Hinges, which was agitated and lifted up much, from a perpendicular to a more than horizontal Position, by the Force of the rushing Air. Whereas in another ventilating Machine, composed of a Wheel with Fans, in a Drum, such as is described in *Agricola de Re Metallica*, and in the *Philosophical Transactions*, a like Valve was moved very little, by the Force of the Air which it conveyed; which evidently shews the great Difference there is, in the Velocities, and consequently the Quantities of Air that are conveyed by these Machines. There is another more accurate Way of estimating the Velocity of Air, *viz.* by holding the Orifice C of an inverted Glass Siphon or Crane full of Water; such as is described, *Fig.* 9. C R I, opposite to the Stream of Air, whereby the Water will be depressed in the Branch C R, and raised in the other Branch I, in proportion to the Force with which the Water is impelled by the Air. When this Crane

was

was applied to the Wheel Ventilator, the Force of the Air, which was sufficient to blow out a Candle, moved the Water in the Crane very little: whereas when the same Crane was applied to the Nose P of the great Ventilators, *Fig.* 3. the Water was so much agitated, that it made large Vibrations up and down in the Crane.

17. Now as to the Velocity of this Wind, it is to be considered, that as the specifick Gravity of the Air, is to that of any other Fluid, so reciprocally is the Square of the Space, which that Fluid moves in any given Time, to the Square of the Space which the Air, by the same Impulse, will move in the same Time. And the specifick Gravity or Weight of Water, being to that of Air as Eight Hundred eighty-one to One, consequently the Air moves thirty times faster than Water would do with the same Impulse.

18. According to the different Position of the Valves, these Bellows may be made, either to convey good Air into a Room, which would drive out the bad
Air

Air at some proper Places, or to draw the rancid Air out of a Place, which would be succeeded by good Air.

19. I Filled the Room in which these Ventilators were, with the Smoke of wet Hay and Shavings; and then, having first conveyed away the smoking Fewel, on working the Bellows, the Smoke was in a few Minutes conveyed thro' the Ventilators out of the lesser Room into the larger Room: Hence we see how effectually they will purify the Air in a Room.

20. I Found that a Handkerchief held near the Nose of the Ventilators, waved and was agitated to and fro very briskly; and a Candle was not only instantly blown out there, but even at twenty five Feet distance, its Flame was blown side-ways; and the Agitation of the Air was manifestly to be felt at that Distance.

21. When it is required to convey great Quantities of Air into Mines, or Magazines, or in drying Malt or Hops, &c. these Ventilators, whether in an horizontal Posture,

as in *Fig.* 2. or standing upright as in *Fig.* 4. may be worked by a Horse, or Stream of Water, turning a Crane, by means of Cogg-Wheels; the Description and Manner of doing of which, may be seen in Number (197, &c.) and *Fig.* (11.)

22. When fresh Air is to be conveyed into a Mine, or bad Air to be drawn out of it, for one or the other of these is to be done, according as the noxious Damps are specifically lighter or heavier than the common Air, then the Box QQ, *Fig.* 3. is to be fixed over the Valves, 2, 4, 5, 7, with the Trunk P, which is to be continued down by additional Tubes, or Trunks, to the farthest Part of the Mine. And perhaps in some cases it may be advisable to close up the Air-Shaft, at the top, with Boards and sometimes at its bottom too, when it is needful to convey Air thence by large Trunks to several Branches and Corners of a Mine. There is in *Agricola de Re Metallica*, not only a Description of the abovementioned Wheel with Fans in a Drum, but also of large Bellows, which are moved by Water or Horses, to convey Air into

Mines: but as these Bellows are made like the Bellows at Iron Forges, with leathern Sides, they will move much heavier than these with Midriffs, which convey Air both rising and falling, which the others cannot do.

23. WHEN there is occasion to convey much greater Quantities of fresh Air into any Place than the Ventilators, *Fig.* 2. can convey, that may easily be effected, by having several of the like Ventilators lying on each other, whose Midriffs may all be moved up and down, by the same prolonged Iron Rods R Z, *Fig.* 2.

24. WHEN the Ventilators lie horizontally, as in *Fig.* 2. then it will be best to have two Pair of them, because they will work much easier than one Pair, on account of the Weight of the Midriffs, which in *Fig.* 2. counter-balance each other, on the Balance R O R; whereas one alone would burthen the Person who moves it, with its Weight of thirty Pounds.

25. BUT

25. But if the Bellows are placed in a perpendicular upright Posture, so as to have the End Z uppermost, as in *Fig.* 4. then, as the Weight of the Midriff would rest on its bottom, only one Pair of Bellows may be used, and those larger or smaller, as shall be needful. If the Ventilators are fixed in this upright Posture, it will be requisite to place them upon the Box B K L M, as in *Fig.* 4. for the more commodious conveying the Air from them; the manner of doing which is expressed in *Fig.* 5. where the End of the same Box B L T, is covered with the Board X Z, with two large Holes at X and Z, cut in it for the Air to pass down thro' X, when the Air in the Side X of the Ventilators is compressed by the Midriff; and thro' the other Hole Z, when by the Return of the Midriff the Air of Z is compressed. In the other half of the Box Q K M the Board X Z is taken off, to shew the manner of the Passage of the Air from the Holes X Z, thro' the Passages Y, X, V, where Valves are fixed, to prevent the returning back of the Air, which goes out at the Nose T Q. The Partition R R is necessary

to prevent the Air's afcending up thro' X, while it defcends thro' Z, and *vice verfa*. The Air is drawn into thefe Ventilators at the large Valves N N.

26. WHEN it shall be requifite to convey Air into fome of the Windings and Turnings of Mines, or to the Corners of large Rooms, as in Magazines, *&c.* this may eafily be done by means of large round or fquare Trunks, made of Board or Tarpawlins, which may be diftended by Hoops or Poles. Such Trunks will be lighter than if made of Boards to move to and fro, efpecially near the Places where the Miners are digging.

27. MINERS obferve in digging a Well or Shaft, that by having a long Trunk in it, the Air defcends in a fufficient Quantity, to make the Air in the Well fit to breathe in. The fmall Ventilators defcribed in Numb. (74.) will be very ferviceable, when the Air of Wells is noxious.

28. IN *Lowthorp's* Abridgment of the *Philofophical Tranfactions*, Vol. II. p. 375.
there

there is an account of four sorts of Damps observed by the Miners in *Derbyshire*: The first is called the common Sort, perceived at first by the Candles burning orbicular, and the Flame lessening by degrees; the Effects of it upon human Bodies are Faintings, Convulsions, Suffocations. The second is what they call the *Pease-bloom Damp*, which the Miners imagine, is the Steam of a Vegetable growing lower than the Level. The third is the most noxious; the Miners say they see in the highest part of the Roof, in those Passages which branch out from the main *Groove*, a round thing of the Bigness of a Foot-ball, with a Film or Skin about it, which when broken by Accident, disperses it self, and suffocates all the Company. The fourth is the *fulminating Damp*, resembling in its Nature and Effects, Gunpowder, or that Matter which produces Thunder. When this takes fire, it kills by Explosion, as Thunder and Gunpowder. The Remedies of the Miners, are by Air-Shafts, and Perflation, with artificial Wheels and Bellows. The Air-Shaft is usually a good distance from the *Groove*, thro' which things are conveyed up and down

down the Mine: And the Air is driven down the Air-Shaft by means of Skreens, which drive the Wind down like a *Wind-sail* in Ships; or by a Fire suspended in the middle of the *Air-Shaft*, it is drawn upwards, as in a common Chimney. And from the *Groove* to the *Air-Shaft*, there passes a Channel called a *Drift*, thro' which the Air is conveyed either to or from the *Groove*. But when the Air in Mines is very noxious, it seems requisite for fresh Air to be conveyed incessantly, thro' large Trunks, to the very Angle or Part of the Mine, where the Miners are digging. Large Ventilators are now making, by a Model which I sent, to be fixed to a Coal-Mine of *George Bowes* Esq; Member of Parliament for the County of *Durham*.

29. In the case of Goals, Work-houses, and Barracks, where the People have full leisure to work the Bellows, they might be placed, either against a Wall, or be fixed breadth-wise to the Cieling, or in any other Position that shall be found most commodious. They ought to be so placed, as that they may best serve several Rooms in their turns,

turns, according as their respective Pipes should at pleasure be open'd or shut by Sliders. And there must be a Provision made, on the opposite Side of the Rooms, for the old foul Air to pass off, in proportion as the fresh Air comes in, or *vice versâ*.

( IV. )

30. AS to *Hospitals*, tho' fresh Air is of great importance to the Sick, yet it must be conveyed into or out of their Rooms, in an almost imperceptible gentle manner: And for that purpose it seems most proper to let it in or convey it out as near the Cieling as may be, where the lighter warm rancid Air of the Room, by ascending up through the fresh Air, if conveyed in, would gradually convey the fresh Air down towards the Sick. And for the same reason the Outlet for the rancid Air, at the opposite End of the Room, ought also to be near the Cieling, for the warm frowzy Vapours of the Sick are continually ascending upwards. Or the Air might be conveyed still more gradually either in or out of the

sick Room, thro' the Pores of large Trunks, made of loose-woven Canvas; which Trunks might reach the whole Length of the Rooms, and be placed at the greatest distance from the Sick, near the Cieling.

31. AND perhaps a like Ventilation of warm dry Air from the adjoining Stove, with a cautious Hand, might be of service to Trees and Plants in Green-Houses, where it is well known that an Air, full of the rancid Vapours, which perspire from them, is very unkindly to them, as well as the frowzy Vapours of human Bodies are to Men. For I have shewn in my *Vegetable Staticks*, that fresh Air is as necessary for the healthy State of Vegetables, as of Animals.

( V. )

32. AS to the Case of Ships, where fresh Air is of the utmost importance, but Room very scanty on account of the great Croud and Cumber of Persons and Things on board, it was more difficult to find a commodious Place where to fix

fix the Ventilators. Dr. *Lee* having heard of them, he first, and then the rest of the *Right Honourable the Lords Commissioners of the Admiralty*, were pleased to send for me, to be further informed about them; and thereupon were pleased to order, the Master Ship-Wrights, and other Officers of *Woolwich* and *Deptford* Yards, to consider of the most commodious Place where to fix them in a Ship. Which was judged to be under the fore Part of the *Orlop* or lowest Deck, next to the Carpenter's Room. And accordingly they were fixed there, between the main Beams of the *Orlop*, on board his *Majesty*'s Ship *Captain*, a seventy Gun Ship; with their Valve-end and Nose next to the side of the Ship.

33. THEIR Dimensions being, in proportion as expressed in *Fig.* 2. ten Feet long, and each four Feet three Inches wide, in the Clear within side; and thirteen Inches deep; one Inch of which being occupied by the Midriff, there remained a Foot depth, for it to rise and fall in.

34. THE Midriff was made of Fir Wainscot

Wainscot Work, with thin Pannels of Wood grooved into four Rails, which run length-wise, and as many across, which were tenanted into each other; the long Rails were four Inches broad, and an Inch thick at each end, swelling gradually, to full half an Inch thickness more at their middle, thereby to give them greater Strength; the Rails which went across at each end were ten Inches broad: In these, about six Inches from the ends of the Midriffs, were fixed the Iron Rods Z R, *Fig.* 2. being fastened there with a Screw and Nut, on Iron Plates on the upper and lower side, which were four Inches broad, thereby to secure the Wood of the Rail from galling and wearing. The Iron Rods R Z, *Fig.* 2. which were flat at their upper Part, being an Inch and half broad and half Inch thick, with several Holes, whereby to pin them fast, into Mortices R. R. of the Lever F G, were, from below the Lever, about three quarters of an Inch square in Substance down to Z, where they entered into the square Iron Socket T Z, into which they were fastened by an Iron Key I; by taking out of which Key, the Iron Rods R R, with the Lever F G, and the middle

Post

Post O, might be removed, or unshipped as they term it, in time of Action, if required: Nothing of it remaining above the Surface of the Ventilators or Floor of the *Orlop*, but about two Inches length of the Iron Socket Z, wherein to fasten the Rods R R again, with the Lever F G, which was twelve Feet long. The lower part of the Iron T Z had a Joint near the Midriff, like two Links of a Chain, or two Eyes in each other, whereby the Rod Z R readily complied at that Joint, which the double Motion caused by the rising and falling of both the Midriff and the Lever. The Hinges on which the Midriffs moved at their other ends, were made as described in Number (5.)

35. The outside Fir-Boards of the Ventilators were an Inch and half thick, as also that in the middle between them which was common to both; the circular Board C, D, D, was a thick Fir-Plank. The Openings of the Valves 1, 2, 3, 4, &c. were six Inches deep, and twenty two Inches long; the Valves themselves, which hung on Copper Hinges, to prevent rusting, were an Inch broader and longer; and their Borders, as well

well as the corresponding Borders of the Valve Holes which they fell against, were lined with a List of Woollen Cloath, both to prevent their making a noise, and to save them from being broken by falling on hard Wood.

36. THE Valves being each six Inches deep, the Partition between them four Inches, and the Spaces above and below them each three Inches, in all twenty two Inches; it was necessary to make the Ventilators thus deep at this end, for near two Feet length, both that there might be room for Valves of such a Depth as was necessary; and also that the Valves, which draw in Air, *viz.* 1, 3, 6, 8, might have full room to move inwards. And that there might be room for the upper Valves 1, 6, to move freely inwards, it was necessary to place the upper Surface of the Midriffs, eight Inches below the upper Cover of the Ventilators, leaving only four Inches clear, for the Air to pass between the Midriffs and the Bottom of the Ventilators.

37. IT was also necessary to have the
Valve

Valve Box Q M M twenty two Inches deep, and eighteen Inches broad from Q to N, not only that there might be room for the Valves, 2, 4, 5, 7. to open, but also as much more room beyond the reach of the open raised Valves, for the Air to pass thro' the Hole L, (there being in this Case, no end Hole P P) into a Trunk about a Foot square, which conveyed the Air near the side of the Ship, through the Gun-Deck and upper Deck, either out, through a Hole cut in the middle of the Gunnel, or up, to its Top.

38. THESE Ventilators were fixed under the Carlings and Legers, which they were unwilling to cut away in a new Ship, till they had been first tried and approved of. But it is agreed that it will be better, to cut away the Carlings and Legers, so as to make room for the upper Surface of the Ventilators, to be even with and make a Part of the Floor of the Orlop; whereby they will not only take up so much the less room in the Hold, but can also more commodiously be come at, in order to repair any Part of them: Here they are placed well out of the way in time of Action. 39. THEY

39. They are worked by a Lever twelve Feet long, by two Men standing upon the Orlop. And being each ten Feet long, four Feet three Inches wide, and thirteen Inches deep, throw out at the Rate of a Tun of Air at each stroke; sixty Tuns in a Minute; three thousand six hundred in an Hour; and eighty six thousand four hundred Tuns, in twenty four Hours; which passing off thro' a Trunk a Foot square, the Air rushes out with a Velocity of twenty five Miles in an Hour.

40. In this Estimate, there is an Allowance made, of two Cubick-Feet and half of Air, to escape at each Stroke, between the Edges of the Midriffs and the Sides of the Ventilators.

41. But notwithstanding this great Velocity of the Air here; yet the Motion of it downwards into the Hold, to supply what is carried off, is so very gentle, that it cannot be perceived; because the Sum of all the open Passages for it, through the Gun-Deck, is an hundred and five Feet square; so that

the Air descends through them an hundred and five times slower, than it passes off at the Nose of the Ventilators: And as the Sum of the Openings through the upper Deck, is fifty seven square Feet, the Descent of the Air through them, must be proportionably slower; besides that a further Allowance is to be made, for what Air enters at the Joints of the Port-Holes when shut; and through the *Hawse*, or Cable-Holes at the Head of the Ship.

42. THESE Ventilators may therefore be used with great safety to the Sick and those who are sleeping, at such times as the Wind-sail would, by reason of the Strength of the Wind, convey Air with too much Violence. They will also be of great Use in a Calm, when the Wind-sail can do little good; also when under sail, at which time the Wind-sail is not used. It is therefore wrong to conclude that these Ventilators are useless, because a Wind-sail will, with some Degrees of Wind, convey much more Air than these Ventilators: For it is not the ventilating of a Ship, now and then with a Wind-sail, when Wind and Weather serve,

that

that will suffice: it ought to be done daily, if a due Regard be had to the Health of the Ship's Crew. For since it is certain, that nineteen Ounces and a half of Matter perspires from a Man here in *England* in twelve Hours; this great Quantity of Vapour, together with the Stench that incessantly arises from the Bilge Water, and from the hot stagnant, putrid unwholesome Air in the Hold, must needs make it very adviseable and desirable, to be almost continually refreshing so bad an Air, either with the Wind-sail, when that can properly be used, or else with the Ventilators, which are intended to supply the Defects of the Windsail. 'Tis for want of being throughly sensible of the vast Quantity of rancid noxious Vapours, which are incessantly exhaling from a great number of live human Bodies, confined in a close Place, that makes many apt to imagine that it is sufficient for Health, if such bad Air be ventilated away and exchanged for good Air, at the distance of many Days, between each Ventilation: As these hurtful Exhalations are too subtile to be seen floating in the Air, many cannot easily be persuaded that such an Air is unhealthy;

healthy; notwithstanding they are sufficiently warned of it, by the offensive Smell; which Offensiveness does indeed much abate by Use.

43. THERE may be one or more Setts of Ventilators of different Sizes in a Ship, in proportion to the different Burthens of the Ships. And in Hospital-Ships, where they cover the Port-Holes with Linnen, which lets the Air in gently, by drawing out the bad Air below, there will be a constant gentle Supply of fresh Air.

44. THESE Ventilators will be of great service especially in new Ships, which are observed to be the more unhealthy, on account of the greater Quantity of sappy Wreak which arises from new Timber, and makes the confined Air the more unwholesome.

45. THEY will also be an effectual Preservative of Horses in Ships, where they are sometimes suffocated, when in a Storm there is a Necessity to shut the Hatches down.

46. THESE Ventilators will also drive out of the Hold of a Ship the dangerous confined Vapour, which arises from Corn;

which is so very noxious, that sometimes they dare not venture into the Hold, till after the Hatches have been opened for some time.

47. THIS Ventilation will also be of service to preserve not only several kinds of Goods, but also the Timbers and Planks of the Hold itself, when laid up in ordinary, as well as when in use; and will make the Air in the Hold less noxious, tho' it will still be offensive to the Smell, by reason of the Bilge-Water, which is made the less offensive, by often letting in of sweet Water from the Sea, and then pumping it out; which good Practice ought to be continued, notwithstanding the Use of the Ventilators.

48. As to the principal Objection, *viz.* the Labour and Difficulty of working these Ventilators, how frivolous and groundless is it, when the Matter is rightly considered; for as they are chiefly wanted, where there is a great Number of Men, so the Labour of it equally divided among them, is very inconsiderable; for if two Men can hold to work them for a Quarter of an Hour, four Men, by changing Hands *Spell* and *Spell*, as

they

they term it, may well work for an Hour. And suppose there be five Hundred or four Hundred and eighty Men in a Ship, and every one takes his Share of the Work; then once in five Days it will come to every Man's Turn, to work at it for half an Hour. And suppose there be in a Transport, or *Guinea* Slave-Ship, two Hundred Men, as there is often about that Number; then it will come to every Man's Turn to work the Ventilators for half an Hour, once in forty-eight Hours; but here, as the Ventilators will be less than the above described Ventilators, so will the Labour of working them be also less. This, supposing it necessary to do it incessantly Night and Day: which need not be in Men of War, when the Port-Holes can be opened, and there is any degree of Wind; which, suppose it be half the Time of the Crew's being on shipboard, then it will come to each Man's Turn but once in ten Days. This Calculation is made on a Supposition that every Individual takes his *Trice* at the Ventilator; but let us allow an Abatement of one Fifth for Officers, Sick, *&c.* then will the Work be no more than half an Hour to each

each Man in eight Days. But suppose it were to be incessant, can half an Hour in five Days be thought so hard and great a degree of Labour, as to render the working of the Ventilators an impracticable Thing? Is not the Benefit proposed thereby, *viz.* the saving yearly the Lives of Thousands, a sufficient Reward for so small a Pittance of Labour? Shall it be said of the brave and undaunted *British* Sailor; that rather than pull his Hand out of his Bosom, and work for half an Hour, once in ten Days, he will chuse to lie down and suffer that brave manly Spirit to be suffocated in a frowzy Stench, a Stench that has destroyed the Lives of Millions of the stoutest and bravest: for the Lamp of Life is sooner thereby quenched, than many are aware of. One would think it altogether needless to use many Arguments, to prevail with Men, to make use of so easy and certain a Way, to preserve their own Lives and that of their Comrades. But I am sensible that narrow Minds, who don't care to go out of an old beaten, tho' very bad Track, are apt to view new Proposals, tho' never so rational, only on their worst side, without duely

weighing

weighing the Conveniencies. This was, within Memory, the Case of a very useful Contrivance, for steering the Rudder by, with great Ease and Safety, by means of a Wheel above Deck. And I make no doubt, but that whatever Discouragement this may meet with at first; yet its great Benefit in preserving the Health and Lives of Men, will hereafter recommend it to the general Esteem and Use of Mankind: For I cannot think that Men will chuse to sicken and die, in and by a Stench, in an old experienced Way, when they have it in their Power to prevent it, by rational and effectual Means. It is well known that all must perish in a Ship, if they will not be at the pains to work the Pumps at proper Times; and should not the same Motive of Self-Preservation induce them chearfully to work the Ventilators, which will not only conduce to the greater degree of Health of all, but will also, by God's Blessing, be a Means of preserving the Lives of many? And let it be remembered, that the Labour itself will conduce to Health, and be preventive of the Scurvy, a Disease which Seafaring People are subject to.

49. If a Wind-Sail were effectual for the Purpose, why do they suffer the Air in Transport-Ships, and especially in *Guinea* Slave-Ships, to be so intolerably nauseous? and even in Men of War, it is well known to be very offensive, especially when the Ports are shut. But this Method is here proposed, in hopes that these Inconveniencies might, in a good measure, be prevented by having a constant gentle Supply of fresh Air, not only now and then, when Wind and Weather would permit, but incessantly, or at least often; in the same Manner as Animals are supplied therewith, whether sleeping or waking.

50. These Ventilators may, not improperly, be called the Lungs of a Ship: And I make no doubt but that they will well deserve that Name, on account of the great Means of Health they will be to its Vitals the People on board. For such Quantities of fresh Air will greatly contribute to make the Air in the closest Parts of the Ship more wholesome, for Sea-Air is Healthy.

( VI. )

( VI. )

51. IT ought in reason to convince us of the great Importance that plenty of fresh Air is to our Welfare, when we consider that the great Author of Nature has allotted near one half of the Trunk of our Body for the Office of Respiration, or Breathing only: can any one therefore be so unreasonable, as to grudge the little Space, these will take up in a Ship, or the small Labour that they will require, to furnish great Plenty of fresh Air? Were an Animal to be formed of the Size of a large Ship, we are well assured by what we see in other Animals, that there would be ample Provision made to furnish that Animal with a constant Supply of fresh Air, by means of large Lungs, which are formed to inspire and breathe out Air in the same manner as these Ventilators do. Can it therefore be an unreasonable or an improbable Proposal, to attempt to furnish Ships, Goals, Hospitals, &c. in the same manner with the wholesome Breath of Life, in exchange for the noxious Air of confined Places, which

is

is rendered unwholesome, by the great Quantity of rancid Vapours, which are incessantly exhaling from human Bodies; and are the Occasion of much Sickness, and of the Death of Multitudes?

52. It is well known that Infections are principally drawn in by the Breath; thus the Fumes of fermenting Wine, Beer or Vinegar, which instantly kill any Animal that comes within the Reach of them, produce their pernicious Effects by being drawn into the Lungs. Which is further confirmed by the following Experiment made by Dr. *Langrish* of *Petersfield* in *Hampshire*, *viz.* He cut open the Wind-Pipe of a live Dog, and stopped the upper Part of the Wind-Pipe towards the Mouth with a Cork; the Dog breathing freely thro' the other Part. Then the Dog's Head being put into a round Hole cut in the End of a large Box, with a Collar of Leather which was nailed round the Hole and tyed round his Neck, to prevent the Fumes of burning Brimstone from coming out to offend his Breath: Things being thus prepared, the Dog received no Harm as to his Life; notwithstanding

standing the Fumigation was so strong, and continued so long, as to put out his Eyes.

53. The Consideration of the great Quantity of rancid Vapours that incessantly exhales from human Bodies, especially where there are a Multitude confined in a small Compass, fully evinces the Insufficiency of any Attempts to make the Air in Ships wholesome, by only a few Hours Ventilation in every twenty-four Hours; it were to be wished that there should not be so much as one Hour without Ventilation when the Ports are shut; but when the Dews fall in greatest quantity, it may perhaps be adviseable to cease conveying the external Air into a Ship, for about an Hour at that Time. Dews do not always fall in greatest plenty soon after Sun-set, but in some Climates some Hours after, as I am informed, *viz.* sooner or later in proportion to the different Heights to which the Vapours are raised by the Heat of the Sun. The Ventilation must therefore be regulated as Experience shall show to be best, in different Circumstances of the outward Air, as to its Temperature of Heat or Coldness, Moisture

sture or Dryness: But that must be an uncommon bad Temperature of the outward Air, to be at any time worse than the inward frowzy Air of a Ship; and consequently Ventilation can rarely be unseasonable.

54. It is well known, that the Vapours which arise from human live Bodies, are extremely corruptible; hence it is, that the Air of Prisons often produces mortal Distempers. And doubtless, where the Air in Ships is much more rancid than in Prisons, on account of great Numbers of Persons on Board, it must needs also tend to make them sickly, and less able to contend with the Inclemency of Air, that a Change from a cold to a very hot Climate causes; which, I have credibly been informed, has sometimes been observed to be the Case, especially where they have been too numerous in the Ship during the Voyage.

55. There is so great a Quantity of Vapours carried off by Respiration or Breathing, that I found, by Experiments, that more than a Pound-weight of Moisture

goes

goes off by the Breath in twenty-four Hours; and that somewhat less than two Gallons of Air, being breathed to and fro, for two Minutes and a half, was so surcharged with Vapours, that I could not possibly breathe it any longer. See *Statical Essays*, Vol. II. Pag. 323, 326. And it is further to be considered, that a close confined Air, in which there are many Persons, is filled not only with the Vapours arising from their Breath, but also with what perspires off their Bodies; which Respiration and Perspiration both together, are equal to the Quantity of half the Meat and Drink which we take in daily; which is estimated to be about thirty-nine Ounces in *England*, and is much greater in hot Climates. And if the Quantity of Vapours which arise from one Man in twenty-four Hours is thirty-nine Ounces, then in an Hundred Men it will amount to Two Hundred Forty-three Pounds, and in five Hundred Men to One Thousand two Hundred fifteen Pounds Weight. Not that the Air in the most capacious Ship can possibly contain all this Quantity of Vapours at once; nor could any living Creature breathe therein, if it were

so surcharged with them: but yet this Estimate shows, how very great the Stench of such an Air must necessarily be; which not only retards Respiration, but also Perspiration, which is very prejudicial. Dr. *Hoadley*, in his ingenious *Lectures on Respiration*, observes, " That the Air itself has so
" great a share in the Action of Respiration,
" and is so necessary likewise to the Health
" and Vigour of the Body, that no remark-
" able Alteration can be in it, without our
" being very sensibly affected by it.—Con-
" sequently, when the Air we breathe is
" loaded with Vapours, which either ren-
" der it too warm, or destroy its Elasticity,
" or both, it becomes unfit for Respiration,
" and interferes with the Action of breath-
" ing."—And he further observes, " that
" unless the Chyle, which is mixed with the
" Blood, be brought to the Lungs in pro-
" per Quantities, and endowed with proper
" Qualities; unless the Discharges thro' the
" Sides of the Vesicles of the Lungs be re-
" gularly and duely performed; unless a
" proper Quantity of Air-Particles be ab-
" sorbed, to supply the active Principles,
" so necessary to the Warmth of the Blood,
" and

" and the Cohesion of its Parts; it must by
" degrees grow less and less fit for the Pur-
" poses of Life: So that by degrees the
" Blood will be so impaired and broken,
" that when it most wants the Assistance of
" the Lungs, it will be brought thither,
" when it is only fit to choak up and clog
" the Vesicles, and capillary Arteries, so
" as to prevent the receiving the service it
" could receive in passing through the
" Lungs."——— Hence, 'tis no wonder that
when we breathe an Air, thus loaded with
Vapours, it should be apt to cause, what are
called Goal-Distempers; which Inconvenience might in a great measure be prevented,
if such close Places were ventilated with
fresh Air; for want of which, many unhap-
py Persons are not only deprived of Liberty, in Goals, but too often even of Life also.

56. It has long been found of some Benefit towards the purifying the Air in Ships,
to wash and sprinkle them with Vinegar between Decks. I wrote the following Proposal to Dr. *Martin*, Physician to the late
*Lord Cathcart*, about two Months before
they sailed from *Spithead* in the Year 1740;
*viz.*

*viz.* to dip many Cloths in Vinegar, and hang them up in all proper Vacancies between Decks, whereby great Quantities of Vinegar would intermix and float in the Air. For I had found by Experiment CXVI. Vol. I. p. 266. of my *Statical Essays*, that an Air, which passed through Cloths dipped in Vinegar, could be breathed to and fro as long again, as the like Quantity of Air, which was not impregnated with Vinegar: so that Vinegar used in such plenty between Decks, might a little refresh the Air; yet where the Stench is great, it can be but of little Benefit, and that only for a short time.

57. VINEGAR has been long looked upon as Antipestilential, whence it is probable, that there may be a Ferment, between this Acid, and the too alkaline rancid Air, which may thereby be reduced, in some degree, from its alkaline, to a neutral, more wholesome state; for many alkaline and acid Mixtures produce Neutrals. It seems therefore probable, that if Cloths dipped thus in Vinegar were hung up in the Chambers of some sick Persons, it might be of service to the Sick. But tho' Vinegar may be of some

Benefit

Benefit in curing in some degree the ill Quality of such close rancid Air in Ships; yet it will still be surcharged with Vapours, which will very much incommode and disorder our breathing.

58. For, as Dr. *Hoadley* observes, "Respiration is best carried on, when the Air
"we breathe is perfectly elastick, and cooler
"than the Vapours in the Lungs; in which
"state the warm Vapours in the lower parts
"of the Lungs, ascend up through the cooler,
"purer, fresh inspired Air: the oftner there-
"fore we breathe the same Air to and fro,
"it will not only be more and more loaden
"with Vapours which, we find by Expe-
"rience, destroy its Elasticity; but it will
"also come nearer and nearer to the same
"degree of Warmth with the Air in the
"Lungs, and consequently will lose more
"and more of those Properties, Coolness
"and Elasticity, upon which the Circula-
"tion of the Air in the Lungs depends, and
"by which the Air is perpetually changing
"in ordinary Respiration. There must
"therefore, in a close Air, be a Time after
"which the Air in the vesicular Cavities of
"the

" the Lungs can be no more exchanged
" for the Air that is new drawn into the
" Lungs; they being both, near equally hot,
" and equally loaden with Vapours." So that nothing but a thorough ventilating Air can be an effectual Cure.

59. AND for the same Reasons, hot close Rooms in private Houses, which many are too fond of, are not so agreeable to breathe in, nor so wholesome, as Rooms that have a due Proportion of fresh Air admitted into them; beside, such warm close Air tends much to relax the Body. It is the Advice of *Celsus*, an eminent Physician, to have large Rooms for those that are sick of a Fever, or else to have a small Fire in the Chimney, thereby to draw off the bad Air.

60. I HAVE observed the Air to be very disagreeable in the Churches of some populous Parishes, in which there are frequent numerous Congregations. Now the Air in such Churches might easily be made fresher and more agreeable, if in the upper part of the outward Doors a free Entrance were made for the Air, through branched flourished Iron-work,

Iron-work, instead of close Pannels: Then by setting open the inward Skreen-Doors, when there is no Congregation, the outward Air would have a free Admittance, without the Inconveniencies that would arise from leaving Windows open in all Weathers: And by the same Means the great Dampness, which is in some Country Churches, might be prevented.

61. I HAVE been the more particular in explaining the Manner, how such bad Airs produce their pernicious Effects, to evince of how great importance it is, for us to use our best endeavours to avoid them. And I make no doubt but when due trial shall have been made, that these Ventilators, or Lungs, will be found so useful in Ships, that effectual Care will be taken to find room for them; and that they will not be looked on as cumbersome, but very valuable Furniture, which will supply them with fresh Air, in such proportion as shall be found most commodious; they being most simple and conform to Nature's own Method of working.

62. AND as to *Goals* and *Work-Houses*, when they have full leisure, the Exercise and Benefit of fresh Air to refresh and cheer them, will, I doubt not, induce them cheerfully to work these artificial Lungs.

63. BUT in *Hospitals*, where also fresh Air would be of great Importance, they must be used with Caution so as not to incommode the Sick.

64. BUT whatever Method is used to ventilate Ships, Goals, Hospitals or Work-Houses with fresh Air, in order to make it more effectual, it is absolutely necessary to use all Methods of Cleanliness by frequent washings, &c. And notwithstanding all these Means, there must needs be some degree of Frowziness, where many Persons are inclosed in a small compass: but it will be much the more healthy, on account of fresh Air and Cleanliness.

( VII. )

65. THE thus ventilating of Ships will be a probable Means, to prevent

vent, in a great measure, those infectious pestilential Distempers, which are too often occasioned by the bad Air in Ships, as also in Goals. When this happens, a very likely Means to cure Ships of the Infection would be to fume them well with burning Brimstone, shutting all the Port-Holes, and covering with Tarpaulins all the Hatch-ways, Gang-ways and Gratings of the upper Deck. And this may be done with great Safety to the Ship, by placing, according to the size of the Ship, one or more metalline Pots on the Ballast in the Hold, each of them having some Wood-Ashes or Sand, and four or five Pounds of Brimstone, fired by a hot Iron Bullet; taking care that no combustible Matter be within two Yards of the burning Brimstone, either above or side-ways. Any one that is doubtful may soon be satisfied, that there will be no Danger of firing the Ship by this means, if they please to try the thing first at Land, to see how far the Scorch of such a Quantity of burning Brimstone reaches. I need not caution that every Person must be above Deck while this is doing, for the burning Fumes will mount with great Velocity and

Acrimony up between Decks, and will destroy all living Creatures there, as Rats, Bugs, and other Insects. When the Fumigation has been over for some time, the Coverings must be taken off the Hatch-ways, &c. and the Port-Holes opened, to air the Ship; for which Reason it will be best to do this, not in a Calm, but when there is some degree of Wind.

66. Mr. *Holland*, the Master Ship-Wright of *Woolwich*, informed me, that he was once concerned in fuming a very infectious Ship, in which many hundreds had died in a short time, with eight Buckets of Tar at once, which gave a strong Fume, with hot Logger-heads, that is, large Bullets with long Iron Handles to them. But as the Fumes of burning Brimstone are much more acid than those of Tar, so they are more likely to cure pestilential Infections, which are with good Reason thought by Physicians to be highly alkaline.

67. I HAVE known several Instances, where after Persons have well recovered from the Small Pox, the Houses have been fumed,

fumed, the Feather-Beds being first lain hollow, on Chairs turned down: And some of the Blankets being nailed before the Chimneys, to prevent the Fumes escaping, and the rest of them being nailed unfolded against the Walls, and all Drawers and Boxes set open: Then four or more Pounds of Brimstone being laid on Wood-Ashes, (which give no ill scent) in an Iron Pot or Pots, according to the size of the House; and placed on some Sand or Earth in the midst of the lowest Floor: the Brimstone was fired by a hot Bullet, or other large piece of Iron laid on it. After the Houses were thus fumed, those Persons who left the Houses, for fear of Infection, have with safety returned.

68. THE acid Fumes or Spirit of burning Brimstone, seem therefore effectually to stop the malignant Ferment of the infectious Matter, that was in the Furniture, Walls, &c. of the Houses, which by a Ventilation of fresh Air would require a long time to cure.

69. BUT the Remains of this Fumigation will not be so offensive afterwards, if

the House be fumed by means of a large Iron-Pipe, or Tube of five or six Inches Diameter; which standing without doors on a proper Stove, with Brimstone and Charcoal burning together; the Fumes are conveyed up the Tube in at a Window; in which way several Houses in *London* and the Country have been fumed for Bugs; neither is there in this Method the least Danger of firing a House.

70. AND as the Infection of the Plague is alkaline, it is probable, it might be of service, if a Ship with infected Goods were first fumed with burning Brimstone: And then when the Bale or other Goods were taken out of the Ship, to have them unfolded in a large Ware-house, where they could be hung up unfolded to their full length; the Ware-house being all the time fumed incessantly with burning Brimstone, to such a degree as the Men employed could well bear: These Fumes might probably prevent the ill effects of the Infection which lay in the Holds, and which could not be come at when the Goods were fumed in the Ship. And when the Ware-house was full of the

hung

hung up Goods, then it would be advisable to give them a much stronger Fumigation, the more effectually to cure the Infection. This is what is done, as I am informed, by Men who have performed a Quarantine, they being then lain with their Mouths downwards in a Room, and then fumed with Brimstone.

71. It were easy to destroy Vermin when they infest a Neighbourhood, such as Badgers, &c. by providing a good Quantity of Tow dipped in melted Brimstone, which being fastened by a *With* to a long Pole, wherewith to convey it, when fired, as far as may be into the Badger's Hole; the Mouth of the Hole or Holes being immediately closed up; this will probably smother any living Creature there.

# A DESCRIPTION OF THE Small Ventilators, And their Uses.

## ( VIII. )

72. AS I was standing in the *Captain*, with Sir *Jacob Ackworth* the Surveyor of the Navy, on the Gun-Deck over the Bread-Room, considering how to ventilate the Bread-Room with fresh Air; there happening to stand by me a Carpenter's Chest with Tools, it occurred to me, that it might be done by a small moveable Ventilator about the size of that

that Chest. And accordingly I made a Ventilator at home of the following Size and Figure, *viz.* Its Length from C to E, *Fig.* 6. was four Feet, its Breadth A C sixteen Inches, its Depth A F thirteen Inches, all in the Clear within. The Midriff was fixed in the same manner with those in the larger ones, was moved up and down by the wooden Handle M fixed in a square Hole, to the top of the Iron Rod R Z; which Rod had a Rivet-Joint at its lower end near the Midriff.

73. It is best to scribe the end A F of the Ventilator circularly, with the Midriff it self, when fixed in its Place with Hinges, because then it will describe the true Curve-Line that it moves in; which will otherwise not be so true, as I have found by Experience, because the position of the Hinges prevents its scribing a true circular Curve.

74. The Holes of the Valves 1. 2. at which the Air enters, were four Inches square; the Valves themselves were five Inches; which will make little Noise when double lifted, as the Valves of the great Ventilators were. The Air rushed out at two other

other like Valves, into the Nose B X thro' the Hole X. There was a like Hole at the Bottom of this Nose, which was a Foot long, and another at the Side: which three Holes had all Sliders to them, to open or shut either of them at pleasure. Tho' the Midriff is worked up and down with Ease, yet it is best for two to change Hands often, which will make it very easy to them.

75. THE Midriff rising and falling a Foot, will convey at each Stroke two Cubick Feet of Air; two Thirds of a Cubick Foot being allowed for what Air escapes at each Stroke, between the Sides of the Ventilator, and the Edges of the Midriff: The Midriff was planed rounding on all its Edges, to prevent its pinching any where. At the Rate therefore of an Hundred and Forty Strokes in a Minute, which may be done with Ease, this Ventilator will convey four Hundred and twenty Tuns of Air in an Hour: And may therefore be very useful in preserving the Bread in the Bread-Room sweet and dry.

76. FOR

76. For which Purpose, a Pair of them were made to be used in the *Captain*, which being placed on the Gun-Deck, over the fore Part of the Bread-Room, Air was conveyed thence, by a square wooden Trunk, which passed through a Hole cut in the Deck, down within a Foot of the Bottom of the Bread-Room; and the Air ascended, thro' the After-Skuttle of the Bread-Room. And in order to try the Efficacy of this Instrument, in the Presence of the Master Ship-Wrights, and other Officers of *Woolwich* and *Deptford* Yards, who were then summoned to pass their Judgment on the Ventilators; the Bread-Room was filled with the Fumes of smoaking Tar, which was in a great measure blown out by these Ventilators, in three Quarters of an Hour's working them; and in an Hour's blowing, the Room was quite cleared of the Fumes.

77. And in the same Manner, the Bread may be kept perfectly dry and sweet, by blowing in fresh Air now and then, as Experience shall show needful, for an Hour in the

the midst of dry Days, when the Port-Holes can be opened, so as to have fresh Air between Decks; otherwise it were better, to have the Air conveyed by a Trunk reaching from the Nose of the Ventilators to the nearest Port-Hole, in order to prevent the driving in among the Bread the offensive Fumes, which are between Decks, especially when the Ports are shut: These Fumes being, as I am informed, hurtful to the Bread, it being observed that the Bread does not keep so well, in Ships where there are many Men, as where there are few.

78. AND whereas the Pease and whole Oatmeal are apt to heat and spoil in Casks, especially in hot Climates, this Inconvenience may easily be prevented, by putting them into a large Bin, with a false Bottom of Hair-Cloth laid on Bars, such as are described in Numb. 103, 104. *Fig.* 8. whereby fresh Air may be blown upwards through them, at proper Times with the small Ventilators, in the same Manner as through the Bread.

( IX. )

( IX. )

79. BY this means, both the Bread, Peaſe and whole Oatmeal, may be kept very dry, ſound and ſweet; and if muſty, may thus be ſweetened. But then his will not deſtroy the Wevels, Maggots, and Ants, which abound, eſpecially in hot Climates, and devour much. The moſt commodious Method that occurs to me for deſtroying theſe Animals, would be by driving the Fumes of burning Brimſtone, both into the Bread-Room, and upwards thro' the Peaſe, by means of the ſmall Ventilators, which may be done in the following manner, *viz.* by fixing a Trunk five Inches ſquare within, to the Holes in the Noſe of the Ventilators, at which they draw in Air; which Trunk ſhould reach to three or four Feet, without and beyond a *Lee* Port-Hole. Under the End of the Trunk on the outſide of the Ship, ſhould be fixed a ſquare wooden Hopper or Tunnel, with its wide Part downwards, which is to be near two Feet ſquare: This Tunnel, and a good Part of the Trunk to be lined within ſide with Tin,

to prevent the scorching of the Fumes of the burning Brimstone: An Iron, Brass, or Copper Porridge-Pot, being to be hung under the Tunnel, about half a Foot below its lowest Part. In the Pot are to be some Wood-Ashes, because they will give no ill Scent in burning. Upon the Wood-Ashes is to be laid Brimstone, in such manner, that a hot Iron Bullet may be placed in the midst of it. Then by working the Ventilator, these Fumes will be conveyed into the Bread-Room or Pea-Bin, and destroy all living Creatures there. This Operation had best be performed, when there is some degree of Wind, to carry away, through the open Ports, the Fumes that will arise between Decks.

80. THAT I might be assured that no Damage could come to the Ship by these Fumes; being very careful not to recommend any thing that might be detrimental to those, whom I have been long using my best Endeavours to serve; I made the like Experiment at home, by fixing a square Funnel, it being the Hopper of a Cyder-Mill, over a Pot of burning Brimstone, with a
long

long Trunk reaching fifteen Feet from the Brimstone to the farther End of the Trunk. And I found by a Thermometer, that when the Ventilators worked, the Heat of the Fumes, at that Distance, was only equal to half the Warmth of the Blood; so that it was no wonder, that neither Paper, Tow, Gun-Powder or double Rum, which I placed there, were fired thereby. Hence we see, that there can be no Danger of setting fire to any the most combustible Matters in Ships.

81. THERE will be this further Convenience in a Bin, *viz.* that whereas seven Hundred and eighty Bushels of Pease and whole Oatmeal, eight Months Provision for a Seventy-Gun Ship, stowed in Seventy-eight Casks, which hold ten Bushels each, take up Thirty-nine Tuns and a half: This Quantity of Pease is equal to 975 Cubick Feet, or twenty-four and three Tenths, Tuns; to which adding two Tuns for the Substance of the Bin, there remains thirteen Tuns, which will be saved in the Stowage of the Ship. Such a Bin will also be much cheaper than Seventy-eight such Casks with

Iron

Iron Hoops. A very little Ventilation will be sufficient to preserve the Corn. It will be needful to have Partitions in the Bin, to prevent the shifting of the Corn, on the heeling of the Ship. And at each Partition there may be a Sliding-Board, five or six Inches broad, set Edgewise; that when any part of the Bin is empty, by pushing down that Slider, the Air may be prevented from going in waste to the empty Part. Or if all Parts of the Bin be from time to time equally emptied of Corn, then there will be no occasion for the Sliders. The Air-Trunk leading down from the Ventilators, may enter at the Middle of the Bin, either in Front or behind. I am credibly informed, that Sugars were formerly stowed in Bins in Ships, before our Sugar-Plantations had Pipe-Staves from *New-England*.

82. THESE small Ventilators will also be of use to keep the Powder in the Powder-Room dry; for a stagnant Air, especially when damp, is well known to damage Powder: And some degree of Dampness, notwithstanding the utmost Precaution, will arise, if there were no other Cause, even from

from the sappy Vapour of the Wood of which the Room is made, especially in new Ships.

83. They will also be of excellent use, to purify most easily, and effectually, the bad Air of a Ship's Well, when there is Occasion to go down into it, by blowing Air through a Trunk, reaching within a Yard of the Bottom of the Well, both for some time before, and during their stay there: This will be a much easier and more effectual Way, than the present Method of letting in Water and pumping it up: yet several are frequently suffocated there, notwithstanding this Method; for as the Eye cannot discern a suffocating from an unsuffocating Air, so many rush into instantaneous Death, thinking there is no Danger where they see none. Now driving out all the bad Air by good Air, will be an effectual Remedy; but however, for greater Security, it will be adviseable to let down a lighted Candle first, for that Air is always dangerous to animal Life, which will extinguish a Candle.

( X. )

84. BEFORE I thought of this safe and easy Method of doing it, I had proposed to make use of the following Instrument, *viz. Fig.* 7. X. Z. a Piece of light Alder or Willow, a Foot long from X to Z, and two Inches and a half thick, both in Breadth and Depth, with a Hole K, L, Q, U, five Eighths of an Inch in Diameter, bored thro' it; and at C B short Fossets with like Holes bored through them; to which Fossets, hollow Reed-Canes are to be fixed, by means of short supple Leathern Pipes, so that they are flexible at these Joints. O, N, and T S, are square Holes two Inches deep, and an Inch and three Quarters wide, with their sole Leather Covers F G, and H, I nailed over them. I, N is a broad Leathern Valve moving on Joints at I, so as to open by the Force of the Air which passes down the Pipe B, K, L, when Breath is drawn in by the Mouth at the Fosset E, which stands five Eighths of an Inch above G, H. G, S is another like Valve, which shuts the Hole at Q close, while the Breath

is drawing in at E; but when, on the contrary, the Person breathes out at E, then the Valve I, N closes the Hole L; and the other Valve G, S opens for the Breath to pass freely off through the Pipe V, A, by which means, the Person always draws in fresh Air. At O and T are two stiff Wires fixed, to prevent the Valves opening so far, that the Force of the Breath, which is but small, could not shut them; to do which, it is adviseable to breathe with some little Force. This Instrument is to be fixed to the Mouth by a Tape or Cord tied round the Head; and it will be convenient to have Cushions at the Corners C and D, for the Cheeks to bear off a part of the Pressure of the Ligature from the Mouth.

85. I BREATHED thro' this *Respirator* for a Quarter of an Hour, with great Ease, when the Reed-Canes fixed to it, were four and a half Feet long. By means of this Instrument, a Man might go with great Safety into the most noxious Air of a Ship's Well, his Nose being stopped with Cotton or Linnen. But I found on proposing the Thing, that the Sailors would rather run the Ha-

zard of Suffocation than make ufe of it: However, as this Inftrument may be of ufe in fome noxious Trades, and other Cafes where it may be requifite to go into a fuffocating Air, I have here given a Defcription of it.

86. This Inftrument might perhaps be of ufe, if there were four or five Feet depth of Water in a Ship; for by the Help of it, a Man might continue under Water that Depth, for a confiderable Time, to rectify any thing amifs at the Bottom of the Well, or to ftop a Leak that could be come at in the Hold.

87. I Know not to what Depth under Water a Man can breathe with this *Refpirator*; 'tis to be feared but a fmall Depth, becaufe the Weight of Water on his Belly will prefs fo hard on his Midriff, as to hinder his drawing in Breath: unlefs it fhall be found on trial, that he can fetch fhort Breaths, by the Dilatation and Contraction of the rifing and falling Ribs; but then, that muft be with a fufficient Force to fhut the Valves. If a Man could thus breathe at fix

or eight Feet under Water, then if a small leaky Ship were put so far on the Careen, as to have its Keel but six or eight Feet under the Surface of the Water, a Man might, by means of this *Respirator*, go down to the Keel, by an under-girding Rope, and there search for and stop Leakages. But if on trial it shall be found, that a Man cannot thus go deep enough; yet he might perhaps go deep enough for Ships, in some degree on the Careen, by means of a Copper Coat of Mail to cover the Trunk of his Body up to the Arm-Pits, that the Arms may be at liberty: by thus keeping the Pressure of the Water from the Belly, it has been found to do at twelve or fifteen Feet Depth. These Things I mention, hoping, that at least they may be Hints, for farther Improvements in so very important a Case, as well deserves the most diligent Researches.

( XI. )

88. THERE is another Use may be made of these small Ventilators at Sea, *viz.* to sweeten stinking Water; and that they will be useful to that Purpose,

pose, is evident from the following Trials, *viz. April* the 21st, a temperate dampish Air, with a westerly Wind, I took near a Pint of hard Well-Water, which had stood in a Quart Bottle till it stank, in order by its Putrefaction to dissolve the tartarine Sediment of Port Wine, which it effectually does. And musty Casks, as I am informed, may thus be cured, by keeping them for some time full of stinking Water; for Putrefaction is a most subtile Dissolvent. This stinking Water I put into an earthen Bason, and placed it at ten Inches distance under the Nose of the Ventilators. After a Quarter of an Hour's blowing on the Water, its Stink was considerably abated, so as to be very sensibly less than that of the remaining Water in the Bottle. And being examined after every Quarter of an Hour's Ventilation, its offensive Smell and Taste was less and less, so as in an Hour and half's Ventilation, it had no sensible ill Smell. Yet it had not the agreeable Flavour of fresh Water, which might in some measure be owing to the Tartar of the Wine; for it is commonly observed, that stinking Water, in Wine, Beer or Cyder Vessels, never becomes

perfectly

perfectly sweet and well tasted, tho' in Water Vessels, some stinking Waters will become very sweet; which is observed of *Thames* Water taken up near *London,* and of other Waters that have some foul Mixture in them; their Impurity, after the putrid Ferment is over, falling to the Bottom, there attract to them all Impurities out of the Water, whereby it becomes fine and clear. And this is the common known Case of Water in Cisterns, which is found to be the finer and clearer for having some Filth at the Bottom of their Cisterns; which Water is often found to become the fouler and thicker, for having the Filth at the Bottom taken away. 'Tis for the same Reason, that some put Gravel with a little Salt into Cisterns or Vessels of foul Water, in order to make it clear.

89. MAY 19th, a warm Sun-shine and dry Air, having thirty-four Days before, filled a clean Cyder Hogshead with *Thames* Water, taken up above the Tide, it then stank very much. The greatest Part of this stinking Water was put in equal Portions into two open Vessels, where it was exposed

posed to the Air, with a Surface of two Feet and a half in Diameter; being eight Inches deep.

90. Its sinking was manifestly abated, after an Hour's Ventilation; I stirred it often during the first Hour, but desisted, on observing by floating Things in the Water, that there was a continual Circulation of the Water, it being by the Force of the Air depressed in the Middle, and raised near the Sides of the Vessel; the higher Water at the Sides constantly descended, and rose towards the Middle, as was evident by the Course of the floating Things in it. And it is the same with the Waters in Rivers, whose Surface having an inclining Plane, the upper Parts are continually descending, which is the Cause of Rivers freezing at Bottom first, which Ponds do not do, their Water having no such descending Motion; but the cold Surface-Water of Rivers, continually descending, it freezes sooner at the Bottom than on the Surface, notwithstanding the Surface Water is colder than at the Bottom: the Reason of which is, that the Bottom Water has less Motion

than

# VENTILATORS. 73

than the Surface Water; for where the Bottom Water has a brisk Motion, it will not freeze at the Bottom.

91. It is this descending, and as it were intestine Motion of River Water, that contributes to the preserving of it sweet, as well as the progressive Motion of Rivers: And in the same, the Upper and Nether Sea-Waters are blended together, by the very unequal Pressure of its Surface, when it is formed into vast Waves and Surges, which contributes to the keeping its lower Waters sweet, which are too deep to be otherwise affected by the Agitation of Storms.

92. After the second Hour's Ventilation, the Smell of the Water was more sensibly abated.

93. After the fourth Hour it was sweetened, as much as six Spoons-full of the same Water was, by standing exposed to the Air, for twenty-four Hours.

94. After six Hours Ventilation, it was much the same as the above-mentioned

Pint

Pint of Water was, with an Hour and half's Ventilation; for this Water being in a Cyder Cask, wanted the agreeable Taste of fresh Water: it is probable therefore, that the stinking Water of Water-Casks, will be better tasted than this, when thus ventilated.

95. THE putrid sulphureous Particles of stinking Water, seem to be the most volatile; for when, in my Researches to make Sea-Water wholesome, I distilled some that was very putrid; that part of it which was distilled into the Receiver, did stink intolerably; but what remained undistilled, was not very offensive. No wonder then, that fresh Air, which is electrical, and strongly attracts Sulphur, should in thus ventilating stinking Water, carry off the more subtile volatile sulphureous Particles, which cause the most offensive Smell, and which are sometimes apt to flash into a Blaze, when Water-Casks are first opened.

96. I HAVE here mentioned the Event of these two Attempts to sweeten stinking Water thus, not with expectation they will be

be at the trouble to sweeten great Quantities of Water to this degree in Ships; but to shew that the highly offensive Degree of stinking Water, may be greatly abated, with an Hour or two's Ventilation: perhaps very long Ventilation might not perfectly sweeten some Waters. For tho' *Thames* Water will turn sweet after stinking, yet pure Spring-Water is not observed to turn sweet so soon. By opening the Bung-Hole, Water sweetens in some degree in twenty-four Hours, as did the other half of the Hogshead of Water, after having so large a Surface exposed to the Air for twenty-four Hours; but yet it stank more than the Water in the other Vessel did, after but one Hour's Ventilation.

97. IF any shall think fit to try it, it may be done without any other additional Cumber to a Ship, than a wooden Trunk, five Inches square within, to reach from the small Ventilators, down to the sweetening Water-Cask; which having its Bung-Hole stopped, may have square Holes cut at each end of the Bung-Stave, wherein to fix the Ventilator Trunk at one End, and a like short

short Trunk at the other end, to prevent the Water's running over, by the heeling of the Ship; by this means, an inceffant brisk Stream of Air may pafs over the Surface of the Water, from one end of the Cask to the other. Care should be taken to fill the Cask only so full, as to leave a sufficient Breadth of Surface of Water, for the Air to act on the Water.

98. THESE are the feveral Offices of the small Ventilators, which a Wind-fail cannot well perform.

99. THEY may also be of use to drive out the bad Air of Vinegar Tuns, and other large brewing Veffels, when Men want to go in with safety to clean them.

( XII. )

100. I CANNOT difmifs this Subject, without saying something in behalf of those, who cannot speak for themselves: I mean young tender Infants; who are often fwathed up in fuch a manner, as muft needs greatly incommode their Breathing, and
consequently

consequently be often very hurtful to them. For when their tender Bodies are close confined in Swathings, neither their Breast nor Belly can rise so freely, as they ought to do, when the Child draws in its Breath: And consequently, not only its Breathing, but Digestion also are thereby greatly incommoded; for the Digestion is much promoted, by the Kneadings of the Midriff on the Stomach, which are no less than twelve hundred in an Hour: And in Proportion as the Degree and Force of these numerous Kneadings are abated by Swathings, so will the Digestion be accordingly retarded and incommoded; the ill Consequences of which, to the poor Child's Health, few Nurses are aware of. Those of them who will not be persuaded to leave off that old very bad Practice, ought themselves to be well swathed up, to be made duly sensible of the Misery they would suffer thereby in one Night.

101. THERE is another very bad Practice in relation to Infants, the ill Consequences of which, few Nurses seem to be aware of, *viz.* It is well known that for very important Reasons, the Skulls of new-born Children

Children are not in all Parts turned to Bone. But ignorant Nurses taking the soft Part of the Skull for a great Defect in Nature, are apt, too often, to attempt to close the Mold of the Head, as they call it: that is, to compress together, by stroking and Bandage, those Parts of the Skull which are bony, expecting thereby to unite those distant bony Parts together; not knowing that the intermediate soft Parts will turn to Bone; and little thinking what Injury they do thereby to the tender Infants, by thus compressing their Brains, and thereby causing convulsive Fits, and perhaps sometimes a great Tendency to Head-Aches during their whole Lives, &c. Whereas, if they would but let Nature alone to do her own Work, the Head would have its natural Shape, and the whole Skull would of itself turn to Bone: And this without Compressing the Brain, which is often attended with ill Consequences.

# AN ACCOUNT

## OF THE

# USEFULNESS

## OF

# VENTILATORS

### IN

Preserving all Kinds of GRAIN Sweet, and Free from WEEVELS and other Insects:

Also, in Drying MALT, HOPS, GUN-POWDER, &c.

# THE USEFULNESS OF VENTILATORS,

In preserving all Kinds of GRAIN Sweet, and free from Weevels, &c.

( XIII. )

102. AS Experiments often give Hints for new Experiments, and farther useful Discoveries, so the attempting to convey great Quantities of Air, by means of the above-described large Ventilators, has led to a Discovery, which will be of great service to the World, in preserving Corn in Graineries, and Ships, sweet and dry, and free from being eaten by

by Weevels or other Insects; by which vast Quantities of Corn are yearly spoiled and destroyed all over the World: I am credibly informed by a *Spanish* Merchant, that not less than 80,000 Pounds worth of Corn was spoiled in exporting in one Year, about eight or nine Years ago.

103. Now it is most easy to preserve Corn, by blowing fresh Air upwards thro it: In order to which, wooden Bars, or large Laths, must be nailed on the Floor of the Grainery, about an Inch distance from each other, if only a Hair-Cloth be laid on them: But coarse Wire-Work is, in some Malt-Kilns, laid under the Hair-Cloth, or Basket-Work made of Osier might be used, and then the Bars may be two or three Inches distant; and there may be the same Distance, if an Iron-Plate full of Holes be laid on them, as is done in many Malt-Kilns. These Laths B B, *Fig.* 8. may be laid across other Laths, A Z. A Z. A Z. nailed fifteen Inches distant, and two Inches or more deep, that there may be a free Passage for the Air under the Laths.

104.

104. THE Under-Laths must come about six Inches short of the Wall of the Grainery at one end of them: on which end a Board Z Z, *Fig.* 8. is to be set edgewise, yet sloping against the Wall X X, whereby a large Main Air-Pipe Y is formed; which having an open Communication with all the Interstices between and under the Bars, when Air is blown forcibly, and in great Quantities, through the Hole M N, into this large Air-Pipe or Trunk, it must necessarily be driven up, from between the Laths, through the whole Corn in the Grainery, and will consequently carry off with it, the moist Exhalations of the Corn; which when confined in it for some time, will, as it is well known, spoil it. By this means therefore Corn may easily be kept for many Years dry and sound, and much better conditioned, than in close vaulted subterraneous Graneries, as is done in some Countries.

105. THAT I might be assured that Air could in this manner be conveyed up thro' great Depths of Corn, I took a wooden Tube or Trunk, which was five Feet four Inches long, and near three Inches square within side;

and having nailed a piece of thin Copper-Plate, full of small Holes at the Bottom of it, I filled it full of Wheat; then having fixed to the Bottom of the Trunk, by means of a short piece of leathern Pipe, lined with a Bladder, the Nose of the Kitchen Bellows; on blowing at a common moderate rate, the Air passed up through that depth of Wheat, with a Force sufficient to raise Paper and to blow off Leaf-Tinsel. I repeated the same Experiment in another like wooden Trunk, which was nine and a half Feet long, where the Air, in ascending up through the Corn, raised the Tinsel also, though not so forcibly as in the shorter Trunk, because it met with more Resistance, in passing through a greater depth of Corn; which therefore required proportionably larger Bellows, and a greater Force: for these Bellows contained but seven Half-Pints of uncompressed Air; as I found by blowing the whole Air which they contained, through a leaden Siphon fixed to the Nose, up into an inverted Glass Receiver full of Water.

106. IN order to find the Quantity of Space there is between the Grains of Wheat,

for

# VENTILATORS. 85

for Air to pass through, I poised a Quart Pot in a pair of Scales; then filling it full of Water, I took the Weight of that Water. Then, the Pot being emptied and wiped dry, I filled it, strike Measure, full of Wheat, first shaking it well; and having taken the Weight of the Wheat, Water was poured in among the Wheat till it was brim-full; when being weighed again, and the additional Weight of Water, among the Wheat, being deducted from the Pot full of Water only, it was found to be one Seventh, and three Tenths of the Quart of Water; therefore the Sum of the Space for Air to pass through Wheat is $\frac{1}{7.3}$ of the Bulk of any Quantity of Wheat: A sufficient Space for Air to pass through it in good plenty.

107. THE Capacity of the Pot being 88.6 Cubick Inches, of which 12.1 Cubick Inches being the Sum of the vacant Space among the Wheat, therefore the remaining 76.5 Cubick Inches is the Space occupied by the Wheat; whence by comparing the respective Weights of the Wheat and Water, I found Wheat to be nearly one Tenth heavier than Water.

108. AND the Air passed as freely thro'

a like depth of Oats, as it did thro' Wheat, and more freely thro' Barley, and still more freely through Peafe and Beans; between which last mentioned Grains there were, on account of their different Shape, larger Interstices for the Air to pafs, than between the Grains of Wheat and Oats; and this, whether there were at the Bottom of the Trunks a thin metalline Plate full of Holes, or a Hair-Cloth: So that the Floors of Graineries may be covered with either of them. But the fuller of small Holes the Iron Plates are, so much the better. But Iron Plate will cost about twelve Pence a fquare Foot; Hair-Cloth not two Pence, which is more than six times cheaper: but then Iron Plates would be more durable; and will prevent Rats and Mice from coming at the Corn, by Holes through the Floor; and are therefore preferable, efpecially in large Graineries: They would also better bear the Fumes of burning Brimftone, than Hair-Cloth, when they were to be blown up through the Corn, in order to deftroy Weevels; but if the Brimftone Fumes be conveyed to the Valves of the Ventilators by a wooden Trunk, lined a little way with Tin, then at fuch a diftance

they

they will not damage the Hair-Cloth, especially considering that the Fumigation need be but rarely repeated. And it is found by Experience, that a Hair-Cloth will endure the constant Heat of a Malt-Kiln for many Years, without being spoiled thereby.

109. Now in order to find with what Force the Air was impelled by the Kitchen Bellows up through the Corn in the Tube A B, *Fig.* 9. I fixed an inverted glass Siphon C R I into the side of the square wooden Trunk full of Wheat, which was nine and a half Feet high. When the Siphon was fixt half a Foot from the Bottom, the Mercury, by the Pressure of the Air among the Wheat, descended half an Inch below C to R, and ascended half an Inch above I; so that it stood an Inch higher in the Leg I than in the Leg R; which showed that the Air among that part of the Wheat, was impelled with a Force, equal to the Weight of an Inch depth of Mercury, which is nearly equal to fourteen Inches depth of Water. When the Bellows were compressed very forcibly, then the Mercury would by Vibrations rise three and a half Inches. When the Siphon was

fixed at three Feet from the Bottom, then the Water instead of Mercury in the Siphon was raised about two Inches, which was one seventh of the former Force. When it was fixed five Feet from the Bottom, the Water was raised about an Inch; and at the distance of eight and a half Feet from the Bottom, It was raised half an Inch; hence we see the different Degrees of Compressure of the Air at these several depths, in the Wheat. Not that the Velocities of the Air through it, were proportional to the several Pressures of it. For the greater Compressure of it near the Bottom, was owing to the greater Resistance it met with, from the great height of the Wheat it was to pass through, which must considerably rebate its Force as it ascended higher; but when it had a less height of Wheat to pass through, the nearer it came to the Top, though the Force with which the Air was there impelled was much rebated, yet the Velocity of its Ascent was increased: for when the same Experiment was repeated with Pease in the Trunk instead of Wheat; the Air having a much freer Passage through them, ascended with greater Velocity, notwithstanding the Compressure

of

of it, and confequently the impelling Force was not in any part near fo great as in the Wheat.

110. Now hence, fome Eftimate may be made of the Force, which will be needful to drive Air up through Corn in Graineries; and as the Force with thefe Corn Ventilators is greater, and the Quantity of Air which will be requifite much lefs than the Quantity of Air and Velocity with which it is impelled, by the above defcribed large Ventilators; fo they may be much lefs, for the ufe of Graineries and Corn-fhips, which will proportionably leffen the Labour of working them: But on the other hand, Care muft be taken that they be not too fmall, but proportioned to the Size of the Grainery; which will be beft known by Experience.

111. In thefe Trials with the Kitchen-Bellows, the Air afcended through the Corn by Fits, only while they were compreffed. But when the above mentioned large Ventilators, whether double or fingle, are ufed in Graineries, there will be an inceffant Breeze of Air afcending through the Corn;

becaufe

because the Air under the Corn being in a compressed state, by the impulse of the Bellows, will, by its constantly endeavouring to expand itself, pass up through the Corn without intermission.

112. THE Air passed through these several kinds of Corn, in the Trunk of nine and a half Feet depth, not only when the Corn lay more loose at first putting in; but also when by striking often, on all parts of the Trunk, with a Hammer, it lay the closer, though it did not, after this, pass altogether so freely, because it lying closer, the vacant Interstices between the Grains of Corn were the less: but all sorts of Corn must necessarily, by reason of their shape, have vacant Interstices between them, for the Air to pass through.

Nine and a half Feet depth of Wheat, sunk on shaking $4\frac{1}{2}$ Inches, *viz.* ——— $\frac{1}{24.4\text{th}}$

Barley, ——— ——— ——— $\frac{1}{10.2}$

Oats, ——— ——— ——— $\frac{1}{5.5\text{th}}$

Grey Pease, ——— ——— $\frac{1}{12.8\text{th}}$

Hence we see the great difference there is in the Quantities of a Bushel full of Corn, when unshaken or shaken.

113. The Ventilators may be fixed against the Wall on the infide or outfide of the Grainery, if there be no convenient adjoining Room fit for that purpofe; or under the Floor, or to the Ceiling: But whereever they are fixed, the Handle of the Lever, that moves them, muft be out of the Grainery, elfe the Perfon who worked them, would be in danger of being fuffocated, when the Corn is fumed with burning Brimftone, in order to deftroy Weevels. The fmall moveable Ventilators, which are defcribed Number 74, will be very commodious to ventilate Corn in large Bins in Graineries; becaufe they may be moved from Bin to Bin, as wanted.

114. If the Grainery or Corn-Ship be very long, then the main Air-Pipe may pafs lengthwife along the middle of the Grainery, through a large Pipe F G C D *Fig.* 8. and fo convey Air on both fides, under the Corn, which lies in Ships, from 20 to 30 Feet broad, and 10 or 12 Feet deep. But wherever the main large Air-Pipe is placed, it muft not be flat on the Top, but floping, like the Ridge of a Houfe, that the

afcending

ascending Air may the better come at the Corn which lies on it.

115. As to the Seams which are between the Boards in the Floors of Corn-Ships, they may easily be stopped, by the Laths being nailed over them so as to prevent the ventilating Air's passing any way, but upwards through the Corn: And if any Wet happens to the Corn, it will drain off well through the Hair-Cloth which it lies on.

116. In Graineries which have large Bins in them, they may each of them have their Laths or Bars to open through the Bottom of the Front Boards: And if Boards be nailed edgewise at the Bottom of the Front or Fore-Boards on the outside of the Bins, they will form three main large Air-Pipes, which will convey Air under all the Bins. Or the moveable Ventilators may be applied to each Bin separately, as occasion shall require to ventilate the Corn in any of the Bins: But when it is needful to destroy the Weevels by Fumigation, then the Bellows, or the Handle by which they are worked, must be out of the Grainery, else the Operator

rator would be suffocated with the Fumes of the burning Brimstone, as already said.

117. But there is one necessary Precaution to be observed before any Corn be fumed, *viz.* first, to drive out all the damp Vapour which is among it; which would totally quench the Acrimony of the sulphureous Fumes: which I found to be the Case, when a cover'd Gutter had the Fumes of burning Brimstone blown in great plenty into it, with my small Ventilators, in order to kill Rats. For though the Fumes visibly passed along for many Yards length; yet they were vapid, and did not offend the Nose, nor kill Animals which were long in it; which was owing to the Damp, which quenches the Acidity of the Fumes.

118. In very large Graineries, there may be several sliding Shutters across the main Air-Pipes, whereby only one, or other part of the Grainery may be ventilated at a time; by drawing up or shutting down different Shutters, as shall be thought proper.

119. If the Grainery be but in part full, then the Air will escape so freely thro' that

Part

Part which is not covered with Corn, that little of it would ascend thro' the Corn; to prevent which Inconvenience, that Part of the main Air-Pipe, which leads to the uncovered Part, may be stopped by a sliding Shutter, or a Piece of narrow Board may be run across the Laths, in Passages left for that purpose: And if there be many of those Passages left across the Laths, it will make a better Communication for the Air to pass freely every way; besides, that thereby there would be more Space left under the Iron Plate or Hair-Cloth for the Air to pass up thro' the Corn.

120. In small Graineries, a very commodious and cheap Ventilator may be made, by making a Ventilator of the Door of the Grainery; which may easily be done, by making a circular Skreen of the Size of a Quarter of a Circle, behind the Door: But in order to this, the Door must open; not inwards, but out of the Grainery, so that as it falls back, it may be worked to and fro, in the Skreen; which must be exactly adapted to it in all Parts of the circular Side of the Skreen, as well as at the Top and Bottom.

tom. But there must be a Stop at about eight or ten Inches distance from the Wall, to prevent the Door's falling back farther; that there may be room for a Valve in the Skreen to supply it with Air; which Air will be driven by the Door, thro' a Hole made in the Wall near the Floor, into the main Air-Trunk, in which there must be another Valve over the Hole in the Wall, to prevent the Return of the Air.

121. WHAT Dust falls from the Corn between the Laths, will be blown to the farther end of them, whence it should be taken out, before fresh Corn be put in, if the Interstices of the Laths are at all filled with it.

122. IT is reasonable to believe, that the Benefits of this Method of preserving Corn, will be many and great; it will not only preserve Corn dry and sweet, and prevent the giving or flakening of Malt, which it is apt to do in lying long; but will also effectually prevent their being destroyed by Weevils or other Insects: for the heating of Corn, is observed much to
promote

promote the Increase of Weevels; tho' when the Corn is kept very close, as is sometimes purposely done in Ships, the great Heat and Smother will destroy them.

123. NEITHER will the fuming of Malt with burning Brimstone give any Taste to the Beer; for tho' I had several Years since tried the Experiment, yet for greater Certainty I now repeated it again, by strongly fuming a Peck of whole Malt, two several Times, at a Month's distance, which being ground, Beer was brewed with it seven Days after the second Fumigation, which gave not the least Taste to the Beer; nor to split Pease which were fumed in the same manner, as I have formerly observed in my *Directions to preserve Corn, Philosophical Experiments, p. 73.* The probable Effect of thus fuming Malt will be, that it may prevent the Beer's working too fast: for this is well known to be the Effect of such Fumes on Wine and Cyder.

124. I FUMED also in the same manner several kinds of Grain, as Wheat, Barley, Oats, Beans and Pease. I gave an Horse

a Handful of the Oats soon after they were fumed; he boggled at the first Smell of the Fume, but eat them immediately. The Scent thus given to the Oats, or any other Grain, will soon be carried off by the Ventilation of fresh Air, up thro' the Corn.

( XIV. )

125. IT is usual for Millers to wash smutty Wheat clean, and afterwards to dry it on a Kiln, in twelve or fourteen Hours, turning it; but then this Kiln-drying often makes it grind unkindly, and not make good Meal: Whereas, after Corn is thus washed, and it has drained off, for some time, the Gross of its Wet on a Hair-Cloth laid on Hurdles; if it were afterwards dried by the Ventilation of these Bellows, it would then grind as well as other Corn; for drying Wheat with cold Air would not hurt it, as Kiln-drying is found to do. And that I might be well assured of the good Effect of thus drying smutty Corn, having procured a Quantity of very smutty Wheat, which weighed seven Pounds and fifteen Ounces; *May* the 26th, at five in the

Morning

Morning it was washed clean, in four several Waters, which was done in a few Minutes, and was then lain to drain in an Oat-Sieve, till half an Hour after Five, when it had increased in Weight by wetting, ten Ounces, besides the Moisture that was equal to the Weight of the Smut-Balls and Smut, that was washed from the Wheat: It wasted but two Ounces and a half by the first two Hours Ventilation, two Ounces and five Drachms in the second two Hours, *viz.* from eight to ten; in the next six Hours, *viz.* from ten to four in the Afternoon, it wasted at the Rate of four Ounces, each two Hours; from four to six, two Ounces and a half; and from six to eight one Ounce and a half, in all about twenty Ounces, some Allowance being made for what Corn was wasted, by handling and biting some of it from time to time. It was ventilated in these fourteen Hours with about Forty Thousand Gallons of Air, which passed upwards through it, and made it sufficiently hard and dry, so as to be fit for grinding; it was well coloured, and handled well, and from stinking, as smutty Wheat does, it became much sweeter. The visible dewy Moisture was

blown

blown off in three Hours, but it continued damp and cold to the Feeling, till two o' Clock, when some little Dust began to fly off it.

126. AND whereas it wasted off much lesser Moisture, during the four first Hours Ventilation, when it ought to have wasted the more, on account of its being then wettest, this was owing to the foggy Haziness of the Morning; which as it went off and broke out into fine warm Sun-shine towards ten o' Clock, so the Air being thereby become dry, it imbibed Moisture more strongly from the Corn. And that this was the true Cause of the Difference, is further confirmed, by a like Experiment, which I had before made on a Gallon of Wheat, *April* the 1st, there being then a very dry North-East Wind: Beginning the Ventilation at four in the Afternoon, it wasted in two Hours four Ounces and a half; and the next two Hours, being towards Evening, but three Ounces; and the next Morning early, before the Air was freed from the nocturnal Damps, only one Ounce and a half.

127. It will be adviseable to begin to ventilate Corn as soon as possible after washing, that the Moisture may have the less time to soak in; for the less the Moisture soaks in, so much the sooner the Corn will dry. The inner Part of this Wheat was manifestly the softer for wetting.

128. AND whereas, washed Corn will dry much more slowly in a moist, than a dry state of the Air, it would be adviseable to have the Air conveyed thro' a large square wooden Trunk, from the Kitchen, where the Air is dried by the Fire: On which account the Room over the Kitchen would be the most commodious to lay the washed Corn in, that is to be ventilated. And in case the Corn lay in a Room, more distant from the Kitchen, the Air might be conveyed thither, to or from the Ventilators thro' a large Trunk.

( XV. )

129. THE first large Ventilators which I made, for drying great Quantities of Corn, were at Mr. *William Knight*'s of Street-

*Street-House* in *Farringdon*. The Midriff rested on its lower Edge, in a Groove which was formed by two Fillets nailed to the Bottom of the Ventilators. In this Position, the Midriff, which was seven Feet long, and three Feet four Inches broad, was moved to and fro, sixteen Inches sideways, that being the Depth of the Ventilators, which were fixed in an upright Posture breadthwise, to the Side of a Garner, which was six Feet five Inches long, and four Feet four Inches broad, in all twenty-eight square Feet. The Laths, which were placed on their Edges length-wise, under the Hair-Cloth, which covered the Bottom of the Garner, were two Inches deep, and two Inches distant from each other: They were all supplied with Air, from the large common Air-Trunk which was fixed at one End of them: which Trunk was supplied with plenty of Air, from the Valves at one end of the Ventilators, V V, *Fig.* 10. the Air being conducted thence, by a Trunk or Box; the Air entered the Ventilators at their other Ends, by the opening of the like Valves, and not at the Valve Z.

130. THE

130. The Midriff was moved to and fro by a Lever, which was fixed to its Iron Tongue S T, *Fig.* 10. and stood upright, its lower End being fastened to the Floor, that being the most commodious Position for it in that Place.

131. When Corn was laid in this Garner, above two Feet deep, the Air was driven upwards thro' it by the Ventilators, so as to raise a Handkerchief which was spread on it, three or four Inches high, and that all over the Corn: But as the Force of the Air thro' the Corn, was something more at that end of the Garner where it entered; so the Corn was laid thickest there.

( XVI. )

132. July 13th, Twenty-two Bushels of very smutty Wheat were washed; in doing of which, when the Corn is poured gently in a thin Stream on the Water, the Smut-Balls having thereby liberty to extricate themselves from the Wheat, swim on the Water, where they are easily scummed off;

off; then the Wheat being well ftirred, and the foul Water let out, frefh Water is poured in, by which means it was foon cleanfed. And then, being lain for fome time on a Hair-Cloth on Hurdles or Harrows, for the Water to drain off, it was put into the Garner, where it lay about 16 and ½ Inches deep.

133. At Nine in the Morning, the Weather being cloudy, with a dry North-Eaft Wind, we began to blow Air up thro' it, which paffed very freely. In two Hours the vifible Moifture was gone, it being partly foaked into the Corn, and partly blown off. The next Day about Six in the Evening, it being clear Sun-fhine, with a dry Wind, the Duft flew out of the Corn when ftirred.

134. The third Day, about three in the Afternoon, the lower part being hard enough to grind, it was turned. After this, fome rainy Days coming, which made the Air within doors fo moift, as to caufe a great Dampnefs on the Flint-Stone Walls within the Houfe, no progrefs was made in

drying

drying the Wheat, not even by long Ventilation; which I was assured of, by putting four Pounds of Wheat into a Hair-Sieve, which was placed on the Wheat, where the Air passed freely up thro' it. Hence by weighing this Sieve from time to time, I found what progress was made in drying the Wheat, in different States of the Air, as to Moisture or Dryness: For the Corn was found to dry fastest in the middle of dry Days, and something flower when the Dew fell in the Evening, and till it was gone in the Morning: But in a very damp State of the Air, there was no progress made in drying. Hence we see how adviseable it is, where it can be done, to have the Ventilators supplied by a Trunk, with the warm Air from the Kitchen. But tho' no progress is made in drying Corn thus, in a very damp Air; yet there is so large a Proportion of the Times, when the Air is dry enough for the purpose, as to make it well worth the while to be provided with these Ventilators, especially to dry cold Corn, which will be done much sooner than washed Wheat.

135. HAVING

135. Having ceased to ventilate from *Saturday* Evening to *Monday* Morning, while the Wheat was damp, it was grown musty; which Mustiness was quite gone in three Hours Ventilation, notwithstanding the Air was very damp. Hence we see of how great service this Ventilation will be to sweeten musty Corn. Hence also we may conclude, that even in damp Weather, the Heating and Mustiness of Corn may be prevented, tho' it cannot be then dryed by this means.

136. Finding that the lower part of the Wheat was dried long before the upper, we took half of it out of the Garner, and then soon dryed it, when it was but of half the Thickness, and the Air in a drying State.

137. *Sept.* 11th, following, in fine dry Weather six Bushels of smutty Wheat were washed and dryed fit to grind, with fifty-eight Hours Ventilation. The Corn thus dried was well coloured, and sold at
the

the Rate of forty Shillings a Load more than it would have done when smutty.

138. It was very observable, that the Air passed much more easily in moist Weather thro' the damp Corn, than when it grew dryer: For the Ventilators required sensibly more Force to work them when the Air and Corn were dry, than when wet: which was, as I guess, owing to this, *viz.* That the Air and Corn repelled each other more strongly in a dry, than in a moist State; which will have the same Effect, in causing the Air to pass less freely, as if the void Spaces between the Corn were proportionably lessened.

139. Hence we see one Reason among others, why a dry Air exhilarates and chears more than a damp Air, *viz.* because a dry Air being in a more strongly repelling State when inspired into the Lungs, it thereby dilating their small Vesicles or Air-Bladders, more than a damp Air will, does thereby cause a much freer Circulation of the Blood thro' the fine Blood-Vessels in the Coats of those Air-Bladders: For, that the Blood

passes

passes the more freely thro' the Lungs, the more they are dilated, I have shown in the Instance of the sighing Horse; *Statical Essays, Vol.* 2. *Exper.* 1. This also may be one Cause, why a very dry Air is hurtful to those who are consumptive from weak Lungs; a very dry Air more forcibly dilating the fine Air-Vesicles of the Lungs, than a moister Air will do: And perhaps another Reason may be, that a very dry Air may carry off too much Moisture from some kind of morbid Lungs. For even the most robust and healthy are greatly incommoded in their Respiration, in a very dry Air; insomuch, that on the Eastern Coast of the Red Sea, when the Wind blows from the sandy Desarts of *Arabia*, they are obliged to moisten the Air, by sprinkling Water, and breathing thro' wet Linnen. And in the Southern Parts of *France*, where the Air is very pure, when it is also very cold, they apply, by way of Precaution, a Handkerchief to the Mouth, when they go into the open Air, out of a warm Room, lest the sudden Change from hot to cold, should cause Inflammations and pleuritick Disorders, by taking in a full Indraft of cold Air. And *Acosta* says, that the

Air

Air on the Tops of some of the *Peruvian* Mountains is so very cold, as at one Inspiration to thicken the Blood.

140. This Garner contained but twenty-eight square Feet: If it had been a Square of ten Feet, as it would then have contained a Hundred square Feet; then a Load of Wheat, which is fifty Cubick Feet and a half, would lie but six Inches deep on it: That Quantity therefore of cold or wet Wheat might well be dryed at once in a Garner, or on a Floor of that size. And Corn thus ventilated may be dryed to the same degree, as any other dryed Corn is, by being exposed in the Ear to a dry Air in the open Field; this sooner or later, in proportion to the different degree of Dryness of the Air.

( XVII. )

141. Millers may very commodiously dry washed Corn thus, and may therefore well allow the Farmer the better Price for smutty Wheat; since when it is thus dried by Ventilation, it will be

be very good, and make good Flour, it not being spoiled by drying on a Kiln, which is the Method they have hitherto been obliged to use. And the more any Corn is thus dryed, so much the better its Meal will keep: which is the Reason why they are obliged to kiln-dry the Corn, which is to be ground for Exportation and Ship-Service.

142. IN Mills, the Ventilators might be worked by a Crank turned by the great Mill-Wheel, whereby the Expence of Men's Labour might be saved.

143. IF a warm dry Air, from a proper Stove, were blown thro' washed Corn, it would much hasten its drying; and if the Heat of this Air were no greater than that of Sun-shine in Summer, it might probably not damage the Corn.

144. THE Quantity of Moisture to be carried off in a Load of washed Wheat, is very considerable: for suppose it were but ten Ounces to a Gallon, as it was found to be in the Gallon of washed smutty Wheat, Numb. (126.) which yet was more, it would then

amount

amount to no less than two hundred Pounds weight.

145. And the same Ventilators might also be used in Mills to winnow Corn very effectually; but then they must be larger than when used to blow Air upwards through Corn. For I have found on Comparison, that the above described large Ventilators convey Air with double the Velocity, that the common circulating Fans, with Sack-Cloths, do. But where these Fans are in Mills, turned with a greater Velocity, than is done by Hand in Barns, they winnow so much the better.

146. If so great a Quantity as four Ounces of Moisture can, by two Hours Ventilation, be carried off from a Gallon of wet Wheat; then this Method will doubtless much improve what is called cold Wheat, *viz.* such as has grown and been housed in a cold wet Season: And will therefore doubtless soon carry off the moist Vapours, which arise from Corn, and cause it to heat and grow musty. And by thus keeping Corn very dry, it will come the fairer to Market, and be much the better for Use. 147. Corn

147. Corn need not be conſtantly thus ventilated, but only now and then. And when it is become once thoroughly dry, then very little Ventilation will be ſufficient.

148. As ventilated Corn may lie thick without leaving any ſpare Room to turn it, the more Corn may be laid in Graineries already built; and where new ones are to be built, they may be the leſs.

149. The Expence of turning Corn will be ſaved, and the ventilated Corn will be both ſweeter and dryer than turned Corn can be; by this means even muſty Corn may be ſweetened.

150. The Expence of Sacks in Ships may be ſaved, or if the Corn be in Sacks, it will keep ſweet, much longer, when the Air between the Sacks is freſh and dry, by the Ventilation of the Ship-Lungs; but this, provided the Corn was not damp, when put into the Sacks. This Ventilation will alſo be of great ſervice to many other kinds of Goods in Ships.

151. Since

151. SINCE by this means Corn can be so effectually preserved, with little Trouble or Expence; it will doubtless be a great encouragement, to lay up large private and publick national Stores in plentiful Years, whereby the great Inconveniences and Miseries which arise from Years of Scarcity, will in a good measure be prevented. And the Price of Corn will not for the future be so subject to great Inequalities, as it has hitherto been.

152. AND this will probably be better both for the Buyer and the Seller: for though in Years of Scarcity, the Farmer will not have so very high a Price for the little Corn he has, as formerly when less Corn was in store; yet he will be made ample amends for that, in selling his great Quantity of Corn, at a much better Price than he used to do, to fill the Store-Houses with Corn.

( XVIII. )

153. THE discovering any Means to preserve the necessary Products of

of the Earth, should in Reason prove a great Benefit to the World in general; yet I should be sorry to be any ways instrumental, in increasing the Quantity of Corn in the World, if by reason of its greater cheapness on that account, proportionably greater Quantities of Spirits should be distilled from it, to destroy Mankind. As things now go in the World, there will in a little time be no occasion to use means to increase the Quantity of Corn; since the number of the People who are to eat it, daily decreases, either by the untimely Death of multitudes, whose Vitals are destroyed, by these hot caustick burning Spirits, or on account of great numbers, whose Stomachs are thereby so depraved, that they can eat little or nothing, to the great detriment of the Landed Interest.

154. If Mankind be thus supinely suffered to be destroyed thereby, he ought in Reason to be looked upon, as doing the best service to the World, who finds means of decreasing rather than of increasing, the Quantity of so destructive a Pest: which is become an inexhaustible Fund of Misery and Ruin to the lower People.

155. It debilitates and infeebles multitudes of the Laborious Part of Mankind; and its pernicious Effects will be severely felt in the puny Pigmy-Breed of future Generations.

156. Besides, the Spirit of Drunkenness, which is now so prevalent among the Dramists, wholly quenches the Spirit of Religion, and depraves the Morals of Mankind. Insomuch that the Reproof of God Almighty to the Prophetesses of old, may but too justly be applied to this Generation, *viz. Will ye pollute me among my People for handfuls of Barley?* Ezek. xiii. 19.

157. This is sure, greatly to abuse that large and ample Provision that kind Providence has provided for us: 'Tis turning into Poison that *Bread* which was graciously intended *to strengthen Man's Heart*.

158. And surely such weighty Reasons ought to rouse the Governours of the Nations, as tender Fathers, to use their utmost Endeavours to deliver the People, committed to their charge, from this mighty Destroyer.
Can

Can there be any Confiderations of fufficient weight to the contrary? And will not this, in the end, be found the moft effectual means to increafe the real Wealth and Strength of a Nation? But what need of Expoftulation in a felf-evident cafe, which ftrikes in fo ftrong and glaring a manner, that not only every open willing Eye, but even the wilfully blind, cannot but fee the Miferies it brings on a great part of Mankind; as is evident to daily and conftant Obfervation and Experience, in thoufands of Inftances.

( XIX. )

159. BUT to return from this important Digreffion, while I was thinking how to make thefe Ventilators ufeful in drying damp Mows or Ricks of Corn, and thereby to prevent their firing, or the Mow burning of the Corn, which too frequently happens in wet Harvefts; but finding this impracticable on account of the largenefs of the Ventilators, the following Method of doing it occurred to me; *viz.* When a Well is made in the middle of a Mow of Corn (as is the known Practice) I would

propofe

propose this farther Improvement; *viz.* about four or five Feet from the Ground, to leave four horizontal Passages, a Foot square, opposite to each other, two of them leading from the Well lengthwise to the ends of the Mow, and two of them breadthwise to the sides; and to make Holes through the Boards, at the sides and ends of the Barns, for these Passages to communicate with the fresh open Air, which would by this means pass freely through the Corn-Mows; and it would also pass most freely up through the Well, if all the Holes are closed, except that at which the Wind enters. Thus, suppose the Wind to blow against the fore part of the Barn, then let the Holes on the opposite side of the Barn be closed with Shutters which move on Hinges fastened to their upper side, which Position will prevent the enterance of Rain, when the Shutters are open. By this means, the Vapours which steam from the Corn into the Well, will be carried off in a manner, as fast as those which arise from the outsides of Ricks, that stand in the open Air; whereby the Corn in the middle of the Mow will be dried near as fast, and to as great a depth from the sides of the Well, as at the outsides.

160. IN

160. In order to make trial of this Method, I provided Cradles, made of four Ashen Poles, which were fastened, at a Foot distance from each other, with Ledgers or Rounds, making thereby square oblong Cradles, like four Ladders joined together. The end of the Barn where the Corn lies, being twenty eight Feet wide each way, and the Well in the middle three Feet across, these Cradles reached from the Well to the end and both sides of the Barn; where Holes were made through the outside Boards a Foot and half broad, and two Feet long from Bottom to Top, thereby to make a sufficient allowance for the sinking of the Cradles with the Mow. On which account, the Bottoms of the Cradles must at first be placed even with the upper parts of the Holes in the outside Boards.

161. This end of the Barn was filled with Barley, in a wet Season, and lain very wet in the Mow, much wetter than they would otherwise have done, presuming that the Well and Cradles would prevent its getting any Damage. When they threshed this Barley in *November* and *December*, the upper part of the Mow was in a good Con-

dition, and, though lain in so wet, the Well and Cradles prevented its heating and Mow-burning. But as it was lain in very wet, and did not heat so as to make it sweat off its Moisture, it grew mouldy, so that the Barley-Ears were covered with a white Fenn. From the Well in the middle of the Mow, to the Barn-Floor, there was lain for Trial-sake, a long Range of Faggots, consisting of three Rows of them, lain on each other: But the Faggots being small, and the Wood straight and even, there was very small Passage for Air; whereas if they had been made of a rougher Wood, there would have been a freer Passage for Air: The event was, that the Corn was matted together and grown near the Faggots; but about the Cradles it was dryer and better, yet this did not reach far.

162. THUS, I have given an account of the Event of this Trial with Cradles, that the skilful Farmers may judge, how far they may, or may not be of service to them in Mows or Ricks of different sizes, and different degrees of wetness or dryness: For according as these Circumstances vary, they may

be more or less beneficial, or even hurtful; for some degree of heating in the Mow is of use to give Warmth enough, to cause the Moisture to go off in a Wreak. It cannot be inferred from this Trial, that these Cradles will be of no service in any Case; for this Barley was so very wet, that without the Cradles it would not only have been in danger of being Mow-burnt, but also of firing. As these Cradles do in effect divide a large Mow into four smaller ones, they will therefore be of use, where the Corn, when first lain in, has such a degree of Dampness, as would be too much for it, in a large Mow; but would do well in a smaller Mow or Rick, and may also contribute to make Corn, which is lain pretty dry into a Mow or Rick, the dryer.

163. I HAVE found on Trial, that undryed Gun-Powder may be as throughly dryed, by thus blowing Air up through it, as in the very dangerous hot Fire-Stoves of the Powder-makers. For, having found, that Air blown from a common pair of Kitchen-Bellows, would pass very freely up through sixteen Inches depth of Gun-Powder, so as

to raife up a piece of Paper that lay on it; I acquainted Mr. *Norman*, Owner of the Powder-Mills at *Moulfey*, near *Hampton-Court*, with this; who fent me his chief Clerk with twelve Pounds of undryed Powder; which we put into a Box, where it lay feven Inches deep on a Cheefe-Cloth, which refted on a Laceing of Packthread, an Inch and half from the Bottom of the Box.

164. JANUARY the 20th, having fixed in an oppofite Pofition, the Nofes of two Pair of Kitchen-Bellows, in Holes made thro' the Box, under the Cheefe-Cloth, Air was blown forcibly up through the Gun-Powder, and every two Hours the Box was weighed, to fee how much it decreafed in weight from time to time. The total Decreafe of Weight, by the Evaporation of the Moifture, and flying off of Duft, and of fome Grains of the Powder, was, in twenty Hours blowing, one Pound fix Ounces. Six Pounds of the like Powder, being dryed in the hot Stove at the Powder-Mills, decreafed in weight five Ounces and a half; hence, nearly half the wafte in this Operation with Bellows, was by the flying off of the Duft, and fome of

the

the Grains of the Powder; which Duft will moft of it be faved, in large drying Rooms, made fit for that purpofe.

165. Now the Powder thus ventilated was thereby fo fully dryed, that on Trial with the *Proof* Inftrument, it was found to be as ftrong, as fome of the fame Powder, juft then dryed, as much as it could be by Fire.

166. MARCH 30th following, the Air very dry with an eafterly Wind, I repeated the fame Experiment, with twelve Pounds of undryed Cannon Powder; which Mr. *Underhill* fent me from his Powder-Mills on *Hounflow-Heath*: it was put into a Box of fuch a Size that it lay 2 and $\frac{1}{4}$ Inches thick. It wafted in the firft two Hours Ventilation near two Ounces: Happening, after an Hour and three Quarters more Ventilation, to ftir the Powder with my Fingers to the Bottom, the Duft rofe in thick Clouds where I ftirred, but not without ftirring: It was well dried in fix Hours, and tho' it was ventilated on for eight Hours more, yet it did not prove fenfibly ftronger on Trial,

than

than that which had been ventilated only fix Hours. When thefe thus dryed Powders, either after fix or fourteen Hours Ventilation were compared, by Mr. *Underhill* and his Clerks, with fome of the fame Powder dryed in his Stove; the latter raifed the Proof-Inftrument to two Degrees, and the former, but to one and three Quarters: the reafon of which Difference, we found on repeated Trials to be this, *viz.* that fome of the fmaller Powder, being by Ventilation feparated from among the larger Grains, its Strength was not fo great: For when we tryed fome of the fmaller Powder, it then exceeded the Force of the Stove-Powder, it raifing the Proof-Inftrument two and a half Degrees, which was half a Degree more than it rofe with the Stove-Powder; fo that it may be looked on to be as thoroughly dryed as the Stove-dryed Powder: It is found by Experience, that *cæteris paribus*, the fmaller the Corn of the Powder is, fo much the greater will its Force be.

167. AND fince the Duft in this Operation did not rife, unlefs when ftirred, therefore it will be beft to avoid ftirring the
Powder,

Powder, while it is ventilating: And as to what falls thro' the Canvas, it may be mixed with the Powder, after it is thoroughly ventilated: There was about a Pound of the finer Corns, which were found under the Canvas, having dropped through its Pores.

168. By comparing this Trial with that which was made in *January*, we may observe, that the different State of the Air, as to Moisture and Dryness, has a considerable Influence, in hastening or retarding the drying of the Powder. And I observed the same in drying of Malt and Wheat; that early in the Morning, they did not waste near so much as in Mid-day. But if instead of cold Air, the Powder be ventilated with a hot Air from a Stove, which is heated by a Fire in an Iron *Cockle*, as is done in some Hop-Kilns, then the Powder would probably be effectually dryed, in an Hour or two, sooner or later, in proportion to the Degree of Heat of the Air; and this, tho' it lay of a great Thickness: And we see in the Case of ventilated Hops, that great Quantities of hot Air may easily be had from a proper Stove. And as it would be

dryed

be dryed so soon, it would save a great Expence of Fewel: And would also be done with much Safety from firing; for the hot Air might be conveyed from the Stove, thro' a large square wooden Trunk, to the Place where the Powder is, at any Distance that shall be thought proper. And that the Trunk might not be affected by the Coldness or Moisture of the Weather, it might be covered with another like Trunk of Boards, at about an Inch distance from the inner Trunk; the outer Trunk to be tarred to keep out Moisture. In this Situation, there would be little Danger of firing the Powder, even tho' the Stove should by accident take fire.

169. AND since undryed Powder can by this means be dryed to such a Degree; Barrels of Gun-Powder which lie in Store-Houses and Magazines, especially in damp Countries, may by the same Means, doubtless, be kept very dry: For as the Liquor in Casks wastes considerably by its soaking thro' the Wood, and perspiring away; so, on the contrary, if Powder-Barrels are in a moist Place, the Moisture must needs soak

thro'

thro' them and damage the Powder. But this may effectually be prevented, if great Quantities of fresh Air be, by means of such large Ventilators, conveyed into Magazines of Powder, in dry Days, and in the dryest Part of those Days. And when Powder is kept very dry, it has been found by Experience to retain its Virtue and Force for above fifty Years. And when once the Magazines are thus thoroughly dryed, it is probable that a little Ventilation now and then, for a few Hours, may suffice; so that the Expence of Labour will not be great.

170. And if it shall be needful to convey Air to the several Corners of the Magazine; this may be done by very large square or round Trunks, made of Canvas or Tarpaulin, which will be both better than Boards, because some Air will get all along thro' their Substance; which one would chuse to have it do, where there will be so great Plenty of it: and the Canvas will last long in so dry a State.

171. And as the Powder in the Powder-Room in Ships, is subject to be damp, so that,

that, as I am credibly informed, in long Voyages, they bring the Barrels of Powder above Deck, in order to dry them in the Heat of the Day; and in *English* Ships, they have the Powder-Room under the Kitchen, as being the dryest Place. Now it may with the greatest Ease be kept dry in Ships, by conveying fresh Air into the Powder-Room, in the Middle of dry Days, with the abovementioned small Ventilators, Numb. 72.

( XX. )

172. AIR is one of the great Instruments of Nature, by the Motion of which, it is not only rendered wholesome, but is thereby also made instrumental in being serviceable to all the Products of the Earth: For it not only, by its Ventilation carries off the great Quantity of Vapour, which perspires from all kinds of Vegetables, which if left to stagnate around them, would suffocate them and produce Mildews, &c. But it also greatly contributes to the gentle drying of the Substance of growing Vegetables, whereby they are not only enabled

## VENTILATORS. 127

to attract vigorously fresh Nourishment, but also grow thereby gradually more and more firm and hard.

173. Dr. Desaguliers in his Experiments on *Electricity* observes, that a dry Air is very *Electrical,* by which Property it attracts Moisture strongly: Thus a Glass Tube excited to *Electricity* by rubbing, will not only forcibly attract little Drops of Water to it, but will also draw a small Stream of falling Water of $\frac{1}{10}$th Inch Diameter from a Perpendicular to a Curve. No wonder then, that Air in passing up thro' Gun-Powder, for a Continuance, should dry it so perfectly well.

174. Having therefore found Means to put great Quantities of Air in Motion, with Ease; we may doubtless in Imitation of Nature, make it beneficial to us in many Respects. Thus it might be of use in several Trades, to carry off the noxious Vapours of the Materials which they are working upon, by a large Stream of fresh Air.

175. They

175. They may also be of considerable Use to publick Brewers in hot calm Weather; when, as I am informed, whole Brewings of Beer are sometimes spoiled for want of Motion in the Air, to carry off the Wreak, which not only damages it, by dropping down again into the Wort in the Coolers, but also retards its cooling; and by being thus kept too long warm, makes it work unkindly in the Tun.

176. I have been informed by an Upholder, that large Stores of Feathers are very apt to spoil, for want of fresh Air; which Inconvenience, this Ventilation would not only effectually prevent, but would also make the Feathers much lighter and softer for use.

177. The Ventilation of fresh Air, contributes also much to the preserving Woollen Goods free from Moths, and would therefore preserve Wooll in Stores.

178. These Ventilators will also be of service to ventilate large Rooms with fresh Air,

Air, in hot Climates, and that more effectually, and with less Labour, than it is at present done with large Fans. And such Ventilation is refreshing, even tho' the ventilating Air, which surrounds the Persons, be as hot as before any Ventilation was made; for Breezes refresh in hot Climates, *viz.* because thereby the frowzy Vapours, which exhaled from those Persons, being carried off, a freer Perspiration is thereby promoted, which refreshes and exhilarates. And for the same Reason, it would probably be of good service to the Sick in Hospitals and private Chambers; if their frowzy rancid Air, (which incommodes the Sick more than many are aware of) could be exchanged for dry, pure, warm Air.

( XXI. )

179. IN order to try of what use these Ventilators would be in drying Hops; I went to Sir *Thomas Hales*'s at *Howletts* near *Canterbury*, where there are four adjoining Kilns in one Building, which have Cockles of cast Iron fixed in the middle of them. They stand on Brick-work about thirty

thirty Inches from the Ground, and are two Feet four Inches high; two Feet nine Inches broad in Front, and two Feet eleven Inches long backward; with a lesser Iron Box, which covers a Hole on the Top behind; which Box is two Feet three Inches long in Front, ten Inches broad and deep: At the Back of this upper Box, is a large Hole thro' which the Smoke is conveyed by Brick Funnels, quite round the upper Part of the Kilns, and thence passes off thro' an upright Chimney; by which means the Smoke of the *Newcastle* Coal, which is the Fewel, cannot damage the Hops. The Distance of the upper Surface of the Cockle from the Hair-Cloth, on which the Hops lie, is six Feet seven Inches.

180. To the Outside of a Kiln, I fixed a Pair of Ventilators, in an upright Posture; which are here described in *Fig.* (10.) I, K, O, O, M, N. They were made eight Feet long in the Clear within side, from A to C; four Feet seven Inches high from A to P; their Depth within from C to D, was sixteen and a half Inches; so that there was room for the upper Part of the Midriff to move to and fro sixteen Inches; an Allowance being

ing made of half an Inch, for the Thickness of the Midriff, which was made of Deal-Boards half-Inch thick, laid length-wise from C to A, and fastened together with broad Battings, which at each End were half-inch thick, but that in the Middle was an Inch thick, for greater Strength; the Iron Tongue S T being here screwed fast to it, about eight Inches from the Top, with an Iron Plate on each side; it had a Joint at the Midriff every way moveable, that thereby it might the better comply, both with the Motion of the Midriff, and also of the Lever G F, to which it was fixed by an Iron Pin, in a Mortice at T. The Length of the Lever, which was fixed at G with a moveable Joint, was three Feet long from G to T, and eight Feet six Inches from T to F, the End which was worked to and fro by Mens Hands, in a horizontal Posture; a small Wheel of four Inches Diameter being fixed to it at R, that it might move the more easily on the Board X X, which it rested on: There were also at X X, Checks to stop the Lever, at its utmost Vibrations, thereby to prevent the breaking the Ventilators in working the Midriff to and fro.

181. THE

181. The Midriff standing thus edge-wise, had no need of Hinges, but rested in a Groove, which was formed by Fillets nailed on each side of it: And to prevent the wearing away of its lower Edge, by much motion to and fro, there were Iron Laps, three Inches broad, one in the Middle, and one towards each End, nailed round its Bottom; which Laps rested on Iron Plates, let into the Bottom Boards: And also the like Iron Laps at each End, near the lower Corners, which worked against the like Iron Plates, to prevent the Midriffs bearing at either End, against the End-Boards, which would make them move very heavily.

182. The outward Boards of the Ventilators were all, excepting the Cover, made of inch-thick Deal, and their Edges well joined with Grooves and Tongues in them; the Cover or upper Boards, were only half-inch thick, that they might the better bend into a Circular Form, in which Form they were fixed by Circular Battings on their Outside: All the Joinings of the Boards had strong brown Paper pasted on them, and those

those of the Midriff on both sides. The Coverings were made of Fir-Boards half-inch thick, with Circular Battings QQ, both to make them retain their Circular Form, and to strengthen them.

183. THE Valves at which the Air entered, were made on the fore-sides of the Ventilators at Z, and just opposite on their back-side, where they could be made very large; for the larger and lighter the Valves be, so much the easier the Ventilators work; if they are between a fortieth and a fiftieth Part of the Breadth of the Midriff, they will do well. As to the Valves thro' which the Air passed out of the Ventilators, there was a Necessity for having them, at the End U U; where, by being too small, it caused the Ventilators to work so much the harder; whence the Air was conveyed by a large Box B, M, N, up to the large short Trunk X, thro' which it rushed into the Kiln: One half of the Stream of Air, beating against the Side of the hot Cockle, was thereby spread sideways, backwards, as well as upwards; the other half of the Stream of Air went directly forward, close by the

Front of the Kiln, and then turned round the other side of the Cockle, as well as upwards, whereby this cold Air was soon warmed: By which means it was spread, so as to pass pretty uniformly up thro' all parts of the Hops.

184. THERE was also another Passage made, for the Air of that half of the Ventilators which was next to the Kiln, to be conveyed by a Trunk, into the Kiln behind. When this Method is used, then its other Valve U must be stopped, by a Stick thrust against it, thro' a small Hole, in the Side of a Box, which is opposite to it. By this means, the Air may be conveyed, partly one way, and partly the other, as shall be found best.

185. I FIXED also in the same manner, just opposite to these, a like Pair of Ventilators, to the Side of the adjoining Kiln, which was eight Feet distant from the other; so that by the Motion of the Lever G T F, which was in the Middle between them, Air was conveyed at the same time into both

both Kilns, by the Work of two Men, who were at Times to be relieved.

186. THE great Quantity of Air conveyed thereby, may be thus estimated; one of these Ventilators, containing nearly Forty-eight Cubick Feet: the half of which Quantity being driven out at each Stroke, *viz.* twenty-four Cubick Feet; this at sixty Strokes in a Minute, will be thirty-six Tuns in a Minute, which amounts to Two Thousand one Hundred and Sixty Tuns in an Hour, if all the Air contained in the Ventilators passed off thro' the Valves: but as some escapes by the Edges of the Midriffs, an Allowance must be made for that; which supposing it to be one Tenth of the Whole, then One Thousand nine Hundred and forty-four Tuns of Air in an Hour are conveyed, which rushed into the Kiln very briskly; insomuch, that if a very thin light Handkerchief was spread on the Hops, it was very sensibly moved. The same thing might also sometimes be observed, when there was no Ventilation, *viz.* when the Wind set so as to blow briskly into the Kiln.

187. But notwithstanding this great Quantity of Air was thus conveyed in by the Ventilators, yet it was very observable, that there was a considerable Indraft of Air, at the Entrance of the Kiln, which was seven Feet high and two Feet wide: for if a Handkerchief was held there, it was drawn inwards by the Indraft of the Air; yet it was very sensibly less, when the Ventilators conveyed Air in, than when they did not.

( XXII. )

188. There are usually dryed on these and the like Kilns of sixteen Feet square, sixty Bushels of Hops in twelve Hours. *September* the 7th, eighty Bushels of wet Hops were dryed by Mr. *Baker* of *Sandwich*, a very skilful Malster and Hop-dryer, in six Hours and forty Minutes, fine coloured, soft, and well dryed.

189. September the 8th, an Hundred Bushels were dryed by him, in seven and a half Hours, fair and good conditioned.

190. SEPTEMBER the 9th, in order to try what Effect the united Air of both Pair of Ventilators would have; by a Trunk of Communication at X X, the Air of both Pair was conveyed into one Kiln; it being stopped from passing into the other Kiln: And there were sliding Shutters made to stop or open this Trunk of Communication when required. An Hundred Bushels of Hops were thus dryed, by the common Dryer, in six Hours, but they were not well coloured.

191. SEPTEMBER the 10th, 120 Bushels of damp cold Hops (it being a very cold damp Morning when they were picked) were dryed by Mr. *Baker*, in eight Hours, with the double Ventilators, fair, fine, and thorough dryed.

192. HENCE we see the good effect of conveying great Quantities of Air, up thro' Hops, while they are drying, and that especially when in calm moist Weather being wet (which is often the case of Hops) they are in danger of being discoloured and spoiled,

spoiled, by scalding and stewing long in their damp Wreak: Now Air being the wings, on which damp Vapours ascend, the greater the Plenty of Air, so much the sooner, as it is well known, will any thing be dryed; especially when that Air is not only dry, but hot too.

193. DID the Wind constantly blow briskly, through the whole or greatest part of Hop-Seasons, there might be a sufficient Quantity of cold Air conveyed into the Hop-Kilns, without Ventilators; for it was observed (N° 186.) above, that when a brisk Eddy of Wind blew in at the Kiln-Door, it moved a Handkerchief lain on the Hops, as much as the Air from the Ventilators did. And therefore it will be of good service to Hop and Malt-dryers, whether they have Ventilators or no; not only to make a large Stoke-Hole or Fire-Place, for Plenty of Air to enter into the Kiln; but also to make large Inlets, on every side, if possible, of the Room in which the Kiln stands; that which way soever the Wind blows, it may have a free entrance; and being, by closing the Openings on the other sides of the Room,

hindered

# VENTILATORS. 139

hindered from passing out again, it will be driven in plenty into the Kiln, or up thro' the Hops: and as there are frequently Winds in the Hop-Season, this Method will be very serviceable in drying them. But in wet and calm Seasons, these Inlets for the Air will be of little service; at which times the Ventilators will be most of all necessary. The having proper Cowls on the Tops of the Kilns, to promote the conveying off of the hot Air and Steam, will greatly promote the freer Entrance of Air below.

194. But there is an Error, which some Hop and Malt-dryers are apt to fall into, *viz.* they seeing that the more a Fire is narrowed in, at the Fire-Place, so much the brisker it burns; are apt thence to conclude, that there is thereby, not only a stronger Fire, but also a greater Indraft of Air, because they observe the Air to rush in faster, through and over the Fire, when the Fire-Place is narrow, than when wide: which is just such a mistaken way of Reasoning, as if a Man who sees Soldiers, for greater Dispatch, running through a Lane or narrow Defilée, should therefore conclude, that a whole
Army

Army could march sooner thus, through a narrow Pass, than over an open Plain, walking only a Foot-Pace. It is accordingly observed that such narrow Fire-Places are apter to give a scorching Heat, than wider ones; the Reason of which is, that the narow ones give Heat with little Air, the wider ones Heat with a greater Plenty of Air, to carry off the damp Vapours.

195. Now notwithstanding this great Quantity of cold Air, was conveyed into the hot Kiln, both from the Ventilators, and from the Indraft, at the Kiln-Door, yet it passed hot up through the Hops, in proportion to the different degrees of Heat that there was in the Kiln; for so rare and light a Body as Air, both heats and cools very soon.

196. Hence we see, how easy it is to procure a great Quantity of hot Air, in order to dry any kinds of Goods with it, by means of Ventilators: for if notwithstanding the great Quantities of cold Air which entered the hot Kiln, it yet passed up hot through the Hops; then doubtless in like manner great Quantities of hot Air may be drawn by Ventilators from a hot Stove, to be conveyed

veyed thereby to any Goods that are to be dryed.

197. I Took the Degree of Heat, among the drying Hops, by a mercurial Thermometer, which was graduated according to *Farenheits*, in which the freezing Point is thirty two Degrees, Blood-Heat ninety six, and the Heat of boiling Water 212. This Thermometer was graduated to 300 such Degrees. I found the Heat of noon-tide Sun-shine at the end of *August*, under a Wall 102 Degrees. But as the freezing Point is a fixed determinate Point; I shall begin the Graduation thence, deducing the thirty two Degrees below freezing, with which this Thermometer begins: And then Blood-Heat will be sixty four Degrees above Freezing, noon-tide Sun-shine 70, and that of boiling Water 180.

198. September the 9th, after two Hours drying with Ventilation, the Heat at the Bottom of the Hops, next the Hair-Cloth between the Bars or Laths, was 120 Degrees, *viz.* two thirds of the Heat of boiling Water. In the middle of the Hops the Degree of Heat was

was 76, on the Top of the Hops, 60 Degrees, seven Feet above the Hops 63 Degrees, it being usually two or three Degrees hotter there, than on the Surface of the Hops. And this sixty three degrees of Heat, *viz.* nearly Blood-Heat, was very irksome and incommodious, to continue in for a time: Much more so than the abovementioned 70 Degrees of Heat, in dry hot Sun-shine: The great irksomeness of this lesser damp Heat, being occasioned, not only by incommoding the Respiration, with a foul Air, but also by relaxing the Surface of the Body, by this damp Air. And the like difference is commonly observed, between a damp and a dry cold Air; the former with a less degree of Cold incommoding us much more than the latter, with a much greater degree of Cold. Now the raising the Heat to 120 Degrees in so short a time as two Hours, proved too great a Heat, especially with wet Hops, for they were not well coloured, Numb. 190.

199. SEPTEMBER the 10th, when 120 Bushels were well dryed with Ventilation; after two Hours and a half, the Heat at the Hair-Cloth was 118, in the middle of the Hops

Hops 66, on their Surface 62; half an Hour after, *viz.* at the end of three Hours drying, the Heat at the Bottom of the Hops was abated six Degrees, *viz.* to 112; at five Hours end it was risen to 117, and was 80 on the Hops. At the end of the drying, which was in eight Hours, the Heat at the Hair-Cloth was abated to 88, and yet the Cockle was very red-hot, much more than any time before, during the drying of this Kiln of Hops. Since then dense Vapours among the Hops acquire a greater degree of Heat than this, with a cooler Cockle; therefore the greatest Care and Skill is needful while they are damp. And here seems to be one of the principal Uses and Benefits of these Ventilators, *viz.* to carry off the Moisture the faster, and thereby to lessen both the Quantity of it, and the Time of the Hops stewing in it. Another considerable Benefit of them is, that they dry Hops in much less time, and consequently not only less Fewel, but also fewer Kilns will be needful, where several are used.

200. By comparing at several times, the different Degrees of Heat, given to ventilated

lated and unventilated Hops, I found that the ventilated Hops at equal Times, from their being first laid on the Kilns, could bear considerably greater Degrees of Heat, than the unventilated ones.

201. By the help of such a Thermometer, many useful Observations might be made, in relation to the different Degrees of Heat, which wet Hops, or those which are not wet, require, in different Stages of their drying.

( XXIII. )

202. I HAVE here given an account of these Ventilators which are to be worked by Men's Labour; because they may possibly be of service in some Hop or Malt-Kilns, to carry off the main Damp, especially in moist Weather, when by a few Hours working they will do much good: but it would be too laborious and expensive to have Men work them during the whole time of drying. It is proposed therefore to have four Pair of Ventilators fixed upright on one end, under a Lodge or Shed

# VENTILATORS. 145

Shed at the back of the House in which the above mentioned four Kilns are; each of the Ventilators to be ten or twelve Feet high, and six Feet wide, and seventeen and a half Inches deep; that the Midriffs may have room to move to and fro sixteen Inches, leaving half an Inch to spare on each side, to prevent their beating against the Ventilators, and thereby damaging them.

203. THEY are to be worked to and fro by the Labour of a Horse fixed to an horizontal Cog-Wheel, as in *Fig.* 11. the Cog-Wheel K K to be twelve Feet in Diameter, and the Arm or Lever I, by which the Horse turns it round, to be ten Feet long, the Drums or Wallowers D, F, to be eighteen Inches in Diameter, which by their Axle-Tree turn the Crank B, whose Crook is to be eight Inches, which will give a Motion of sixteen Inches to and fro to the Midriffs, by means of a Rod or Pole fixed to the Crank and to the Lever at F or G, *Fig.* 4.

204. AND the Crank must be made to be turned by the Axle-Tree of the Wallowers or not, at pleasure, by means of a

L  square

square Iron-Box C or E; which by sliding on or off, is made to take hold of the square end of the Axle-Tree, on which the Drum-Wallower turns.

205. For as the great Cog-Wheel, by standing in the middle between the four Ventilators, is to have a Wallower and Crank of each side; so by means of these sliding Iron-Boxes, either all the Ventilators may be worked at the same time, or only two Pair of them, as occasion shall require.

206. The Crooks of the Cranks when working must not stand both the same way; but they must be so fixed by the sliding Iron-Boxes, that when one of the Crooks is at the top or bottom of its Circle, the other must be side-ways, directly at right Angles to each other. This Position will prevent the heaviest and most laborious Parts, in the Motion of each Crank, from coming together, which will make it the easier for the Horse to turn them. The Air to be conveyed thence through Valves and Passages formed in the same manner as those in *Fig.* 4, and 5.

207.

207. G is a Section of the main Beam in which the Gudgeons of the Axle-Trees of the great Cog-Wheel, and of the two Wallowers do turn; the Gudgeons of their other ends being at A, &c.

208. The Ventilators must stand about fourteen Inches from the Wall of the House, that there may be room for Trunks of a Foot square within, which are to lead thro' to the back of the Kilns, and also to leave room for large Valves for the Air to enter the Ventilators, of seven Inches depth, and two Feet long.

209. But the Air of both Pair of Ventilators is not to pass in this Case, as in *Fig.* 5 at T Q, into one common Trunk; but it is to pass out at B L K M, *Fig.* 4. near their outsides, into separate Trunks behind; each pair of Ventilators being to supply their respective Kiln with Air. The other Wallower F is to turn another Crank, which is to work the two other Ventilators.

210. Now to make some Estimate of the great Quantities of Air, which will thereby be conveyed into each of the four Kilns: It is found by Experience that Horses, one with another, can draw a Force equal to 200 Pounds weight, for eight Hours in a Day; walking at the rate of about two Miles, and three Tenths, in an Hour; which is about three Feet and a half in a Second of Time, or the sixtieth part of a Minute. And if the same Horse is made to draw 240 Pounds, he can work but six Hours in a Day; and cannot go quite so fast. See Dr. *Desaguliers's Course of Experimental Philosophy*, p. 241. And p. 243, he says he has found, that five Men are equal in Strength to one Horse, and can with the same Ease push round the horizontal Arm, in a Walk of forty Feet Diameter; which he says, should never be less, where there is room for it; that being much easier for a Horse to walk in, than a nineteen-Feet Walk: For he observes, that three Men will push round an Arm, in a 19 Feet Walk, which an Horse, otherwise equal to five Men, can but draw round. But though a 40 Feet Walk would be

be better for the Horse, than one of 19 Feet, on account of his turning continually too short; yet in this Case there is a Necessity for using the latter, because the former would make the Lodge too large. A Man of 140 Pounds Weight drawing a Boat, by a Rope coming over his Shoulders, cannot draw above 27 Pounds, which is about one seventh Part of what a Horse can draw in that Case. *ib.*

211. SINCE then a Horse can walk, drawing for eight Hours 200 Weight, at the rate of two Miles and three Tenths, or 12600 Feet in an Hour; which will make in his Circumference of 57 Feet (allowing the Diameter of his Walk to be 19 Feet) 222 Revolutions in an Hour: And the great horizontal Cog-Wheel being 36 Feet in Circumference, its Circumference goes round at the rate of 7992 Feet in an Hour; which divided by four, the Circumference of the Wallower at its Rounds or Cogs, gives 1998 Revolutions of the Cranks in an Hour, which is at the rate of 33 Revolutions in a Minute.

212. WHICH supposing the Ventilators to be each ten Feet high and five Feet wide, will be twenty two and a half Feet of Air at a Stroke, allowing as above (Numb. 186) one Tenth of the Air to escape at the Edges of the Midriffs; and each Revolution of the Cranks giving two Strokes, that will be sixty six in a Minute, and two Thousand two Hundred and twenty seven Tuns, which each of the four Ventilators will convey into each Kiln in an Hour; that is 283 Tuns more than the Hand-Ventilators Numb. 186. do convey, in the same Time. And if these Ventilators are made 12 Feet high, and six Feet wide, then the Quantity of Air conveyed into each Kiln, will be 3207 Tuns in an Hour. These very large Horse-Ventilators will therefore be of service, where it is needful to convey very great Quantities of Air, as here in this Case, and in very large Mines, &c. where the Air conveyed by two pair of them, as in *Fig.* 2. or 4. will be at the rate of 6414 Tuns in an Hour.

(XXIV.)

( XXIV. )

213. WHEN Hops, especially wet ones, lie many Hours in a Heap, before they are laid on the Kilns to dry; they are apt to get Damage, and be difcoloured. To prevent which Inconvenience, I fixed in the fame Hop-Houfe two Pair of fuch Ventilators, as are defcribed in *Fig.* 2. to the Joice, which bear up the Floor on which the green Hops are laid; they were feven Feet eight Inches long, and four Feet four Inches broad, and twelve and a half Inches deep within fide; fo there was room for the Midriffs to move up and down a Foot: But at the other Valve end, they were twenty Inches deep, for the fake of the larger Valves, which were each fourteen Inches long, and eight deep: One Inch of the Subftance of the Valve-Board being left at the Top, two in the middle, and one at the Bottom, for the Valves to be nailed to and fall againft.

214. FROM thefe Valves the Air was conveyed

conveyed in and out of the Ventilators at the rate of about 2712 Tuns in an Hour, up into a large Air-Trunk, which was fifteen Feet long, whence it run between wooden Bars nailed on the Floor, which were four Inches deep, two Inches thick, and two Inches distant from each other: But it had taken up much less Stuff, if Laths or Bars only two Inches thick had been nailed on the Floor, at the Distance of fifteen Inches; and across them, other Laths, at two Inches distance, as described in *Fig.* 8. On these was laid a Hair-Cloth seventeen Feet long, and fifteen broad.

215. WHEN the Ventilators were worked, which was done by means of another Lever fixed sideways, like a Pump-Handle to one end G or F of the long Lever, *Fig.* 2. then a Handkerchief, which was spread on the Hair-Cloth, was blown up several Inches; but not so, at those Parts which were far from the great Air-Trunk Z X Y, *Fig.* 8. *viz.* because the Air passing most freely through the Hair-Cloth, was all wasted, long before it reached to the farther end; for which reason, the Air passing also very

freely

freely through Hops, they ought to be laid four or five times thicker, near the great Air-Trunk, than at the farther end; where the Interstices of the Bars were closed up with a Board, and pasted with Paper, as were also all the Joints of the Boards of the Floor, to prevent the escaping of Air.

216. These Ventilators will be of use not only for preserving of Hops, but also for drying cold, and sweetening musty Corn. With a view to which, a sliding Shutter was fixed in the great Air-Trunk Z Z, to stop its ascending up through the whole Hair-Cloth, in case one Part of it shall be sufficient for the Quantity of Corn that is to be ventilated; for the less the Spread of the Hair-Cloth, so much the faster will the Air pass up thro' it.

( XXV. )

217. AS to Malt, being desirous to try, what Degree of Dryness might be given it, by being ventilated upwards with common cold Air; *March* 22d, there being a dry North-East Wind, I procured a Pack of

of undryed Malt, and put it into a Box, with a Canvas falfe Bottom, where it lay about four Inches thick. It weighed 8 Pounds, 7 Ounces and a half, and one Dram. During the firſt ſix Hours Ventilation upwards, it waſted at the rate of three Ounces and a half every two Hours; during the following fifty Hours Ventilation, it waſted nearly at the rate of one Ounce and a half every two Hours; and for the remaining laſt twelve Hours, it waſted nearly at the rate of half an Ounce every two Hours. So that in ſixty eight Hours, it waſted in all four Pounds, twelve Ounces and a half, *viz.* near $\frac{1}{7}$ of the whole weight: in which time there paſſed through the Interſtices of the Malt 244,000 Gallons of Air. This Malt when thus dryed was criſp and hard to bite, but not near ſo hard as Kiln-dryed pale Malt, which is 24 Hours in drying: on which account it did not grind ſo well, and ſome of it, tho' cloſe corked up in a Bottle, did after ſome days grow leſs hard, *viz.* probably becauſe the Moiſture near the middle diffuſed itſelf towards the dryer and harder outſide. Ale was brewed with this Malt, which was very well taſted, but not ſo pale as was expected; which

which might be owing to the manner of preparing it in the Couch.

218. But if inſtead of cold, plenty of hot Air be conveyed upwards through Malt, it will then dry, not only much faſter, but alſo better than in the common way of drying. For when, for trial, pale Malt was dryed, on one of the abovementioned Kilns, Numb. 179. and ventilated, the firſt Kiln was dryed in eleven Hours, and a ſecond Kiln in nine Hours; during eight Hours of which nine, the drying Malt was ventilated: whereas a like Kiln of unventilated Malt was at the ſame time twenty Hours in drying, the Wind blowing very freſh; whereby, the more Air being conveyed in at the Kiln-Door, brought it on ſooner than it would otherwiſe have done; a Kiln of Pale Malt being uſually about twenty-four Hours in drying and hardening.

219. The abovementioned Mr. *Baker* obſerved, that though the Weather was wet, and the Tiles very damp within, yet the Moiſture went off the Malt, without Sweat, with Ventilation, in much leſs Time, than in the other Kiln without Ventilation, which

which sweat very much; and consequently the Malt which was dryed without Sweat, was much the better of the two. This Malt, he says, was very good, being dryed pale, and made a pale Wort of a fine Taste. Though he observes, that it will not be so pale with a Cockle-Kiln, as when dryed in an open Kiln, with Coake, or *Welch* Coal.

220. ONE Pair of these Ventilators being given him, he conveyed them to *Sandwich*, and fixed them to his open Malt-Kiln there, which had no Cockle in it: where he found that by Ventilation, he could dry either pale or brown Malt, in half the usual Time, with a somewhat larger Fire; for as in drying Hops, so in drying Malt, a greater Heat may be given when ventilated, than when not. And the pale Malt thus dryed, was paler and lower coloured, and the brown much brighter, than that which is dryed without Ventilation: Whence he concludes, that both sorts being thus dryed without Sweat, will make better Beer, than if dryed in the usual Way.

221. IF the Labour of working the Ventilators, during the whole time of drying,

shall be thought too much; he is of Opinion, that it would do good Service, if they were worked only so long, as the principal Damp continued among the Malt; especially in a still, moist, heavy Air.

222. HE observed, that Malt lying closer together than Hops, a light Handkerchief laid on it, was not so sensibly moved by Ventilation, as when it lay spread on Hops.

223. THE usual Heat given to pale Malt, which is to be dryed in twenty-four Hours, is about fifty-two Degrees above freezing, which is twelve Degrees, *viz.* near one Sixth below Blood-warm: But when towards the latter End of drying, the principal Moisture is gone off, then the Heat of the Malt is increased to 138 Degrees above Freezing, *viz.* more than double the Heat of Blood, which is 64 Degrees. And this Degree of Heat both hardens the Malt, so as to make it keep long well in Store, and also gives it an agreeable Sweetness.

224. IN order to make brown Malt, a
much

much greater degree of Heat is given it, while it is in a damp Sweat.

## ( XXVI. )

225. THESE Ventilators may also be of use to those who take the Hulls off from any Grains, by moistening them first: Thus whited Pepper may be well dryed; and Starch-Makers may thus dry their Starch, with warm Air from a Stove. Several kinds of Sweatmeats may be dryed thus, and also be preserved very dry and free from Damp or Mouldiness, by ventilating them now and then for a little time.

226. AND if the frowzy Air of *Larders*, *Pantreys*, and *Safes*, be now and then thus exchanged for fresh Air, it will contribute to the keeping of the Meat sweet, and free from Mustiness, much the longer.

227. AND since a moist Air conduces much to the rusting of Iron, they would probably be very serviceable, in keeping Arms bright in large Armories, such as are in the *Tower* of *London*.

228. THE

228. The Expence of Trial with these Ventilators in these Cases, is inconsiderable, and the Benefit proposed great. They will doubtless also be of service in many other Instances, which do not occur to me, but may hereafter be thought of, and applied by others to be serviceable to them in their several Professions.

( XXVII. )

229. IF I had had Opportunities to make more Trials in several of the Things here proposed, I could have given a fuller and more satisfactory Account of them. It were therefore to be wished, that whatever Success or Difficulties occur on trial, as also what further Improvements shall hereafter be made herein, were from time to time communicated to the World.

230. It will be a great Satisfaction to me, if these Things shall prove beneficial to Mankind; especially to those numerous, useful and valuable Persons, *who occupy their Business in great Waters:* Whom I have laboured

in many ways to do the best Service I could. And oh! that I could prevail with them, to be in earnest so true to their own Interest, as not to destroy their Health and shorten their Lives, by the intemperate Use of distilled spirituous Liquors, such as Brandy, Rum, Arrack, &c. The Health of many of them is impaired, and dangerous Sicknesses are often occasioned, by the very noxious rancid close Air in Ships: But the Number of those, who lose their Lives by this, and all other Dangers and Difficulties they are exposed to, is small in comparison of the vast Multitudes that are destroyed by these pernicious Liquors, especially in hot Climates. And will not the yearly Destruction of Thousands, nay of Millions all over the World, deter them from it? Will not the strong natural Desire they have to *live long and see good* and healthy *Days*, prevail with them to avoid this Bane of Mankind? Will they, in spite of all these Arguments, be their own Executioners, and consign themselves over, not only to present, but eternal Death also?

# ON SHIP-WORMS.

## ( XXVIII. )

231. IT may not be improper here to mention a Proposal which I have long thought might probably prove of very great Service to Shipping: And that is, to have a short Account drawn up and published of the principal Methods, that are now in use, or that have from time to time been proposed and tryed; for preventing the Planks and Timbers of Ships being eaten by Worms. This seems to me, to be the likeliest Way to find out a more effectual and cheaper Remedy than is yet known. Were I to engage in the Research, which I have no Intention to do; I should, in the first place, make it my Endeavour, to know what had hitherto been attempted; and the Reasons why those several Attempts had proved unsuccessful:

successful: for I have frequently found, that the knowing what will not do, has led me to the thing sought after. The Mind unassisted, can view but one Thing at a time; but when all the several Attempts are laid before it, in one View, they may give rise to new Hints; or various Combinations, of some of those Things which alone have proved unsuccessful, may perhaps be more effectual.

232. AND besides, by setting the Thing in a clear and full View, to the World; it will very much increase the Probability of Success: for as Men have very different Views of Things according to their different Talents, or Professions; so that what may never be discovered by very ingenious Men in one Profession, may yet haply be done by others. Thus, if Artizans of different Professions would consult each other, and if those who have a more inlarged Knowledge of Nature would consult Artizans, and Artizans them, and each openly and candidly communicate Notices to each other, there would doubtless by this means

be

be many useful Discoveries made from time to time, to the great Benefit of Mankind.

233. I Cannot therefore forbear heartily to recommend the Thing not only to my own Country, but to all Maritime Nations, that they would join in communicating their several Attempts in this way; and if withal a Reward was annexed, I believe a much less Reward than what is offered for the Discovery of the Longitude, would spur People on to engage in a Research; which, as it is of vastly more Importance to Navigation, than the Discovery of the Longitude; so, for our Encouragement, there is a much greater Probability of Success in it. As several ingenious Persons have made considerable useful Advances, in that less important, and probably more difficult Discovery; so there is good reason to think that very useful Improvements would in a little Time be made in this.

234. I Shall only mention, that, from some Observations which I have made, it is to be feared, that oily unctuous Things are not likely to penetrate deep into Oak,

which has a watry Sap: But, as it is well known to Oilmen, it will penetrate far into Fir, which has an oily unctuous Sap, Oil and Oil readily uniting; insomuch, that they are obliged to set Vessels under the Fir Heads of Oil-Casks, to receive the Droppings of Oil which ouze thro' the whole Substance of the Wood, tho' thick. And they further observe, that Oil gives the Fir such a surprizing Degree of Toughness, as will turn the Edge of the Adze or Ax, in cutting it: Now if Oil could be made thus to penetrate into the Substance of the Fir-Boards with which Ships are sheathed; and there were mixed with the Oil, some proper Thing that were disagreeable to the Worms, then this would preserve the Ships: But in case that neither such a Mixture nor the Oil could be made to penetrate deep into the Fir, yet as frequent oiling would give great Toughness and Dureableness to the Sheathing; so such Sheathing would so much the longer preserve such a *Paying* under it, from being rubbed off, as should be found impenetrable to the Worms; and that such Payings may be had, there is no doubt; but the great Difficulty has hitherto been, as I am informed, to preserve

preserve such Paying from being rubbed off.

235. As Verdigrease is most disagreeable and destructive to all Animals whatsoever; so I believe that a very small Proportion of it in any Paying whatever, would do good Service. I have found, that a thirtieth Part of it melted with Tallow, has given the Tallow a considerable degree of Greenness: and also that Sea-Water will not wash it out of the Tallow, even tho' it has laid long in it, and coarse Verdigrease is not dear.

236. THE great Damage that is done to Shipping by Worms, as it has doubtless hitherto put Men on trying from time to time, all imaginable Means to prevent it; so should it urge us on, still to persevere, and not despair of Success, in so important an Affair.

*FINIS.*

# A GENERAL INDEX OF THE *Matters contained in this Book.*

### A.

AIR, *a Tun weighs 300 Grains,* 3.
*The Quantity we breathe in 24 Hours,* 3.
*The Quantity conveyed by Ventilators,* 12, 30, 148.
*Its Velocity estimated,* 12, &c. 30.
*In Ships unwholesome,* 32.
*Bad, its pernicious Effects,* 42, *to* 50.
*Its suffocating Power to prove,* 65.
*Dry, best to Ventilate Corn,* 98, &c. 123.
*Dry, its Effect on Respiration,* 106.
*One of the great Instruments of Nature,* 126.
*Is electrical,* 127.

# INDEX.

Air, *hot, to convey in plenty,* 140.
Armories, *to be ventilated,* 158.

### B.

Barracks, *to ventilate,* 22.
Beer, *hot, to cool by Ventilation,* 128.
Bins, *proposed to preserve Peaſe in Ships,* 60, 61.
　*By them much Stowage ſaved,* 63.
Bottles, *to clean,* 70.
Bread, *in Ships to preſerve,* 59, 69.
Breath, *draws Infections in,* 40.
　*The Quantity carried off by it,* 43.
　*How incommoded,* 44, 47.
　*In cloſe Rooms,* 48.
Brimſtone, *its Fumes cure Infection,* 51, 52.
Bugs, *to deſtroy,* 53, 54.

### C.

Casks, *muſty, to ſweeten,* 70.
Churches, *their Air to refreſh,* 48.
Cleanlineſs, *withal recommended,* 50.
Corn, *in Ships to ventilate,* 33, 91, 92.
　*To preſerve,* 81, &c.
　*How much it ſhrinks in Meaſure on ſhaking,* 90.
　*To fumigate,* 93.
　*Fumigated has no ill Savour,* 96.
　*Waſhed, ventilated dry,* 97, 102, &c.
　*Muſty to ſweeten,* 105.

Corn,

Corn, *in Graineries and Ships to ventilate,* 111.
  *In Mows to dry,* 115.

### D.

Damps, *their kinds in Mines,* 21.
A Diving *Instrument described,* 66.
Drams, *their pernicious Effects,* 112.

### F.

Fir, *imbibes Oil,* 164.
Fumigation, *proposed to cure Ships and Houses of Infection,* 51, 52.
  *To preserve Bread and Pease in Ships,* 61, 62.
  *Of Corn,* 93.
  *Gives Corn no ill Savour,* 96.

### G.

Goals, *to ventilate,* 22, 50.
  *Distempers,* 45.
Graineries, *how to prepare,* 82, 91, &c.
  *To ventilate now and then,* 111.
  *The great Use of ventilating them,* 112.
Green-Houses, *to ventilate,* 24.
Gun-Powder, *kept dry by Ventilation,* 64, 124, 125.
  *To dry,* 119.

### H.

Hops, *Kilns to order,* 138.
  *Ventilators,* 129, 144.
  *To ventilate,* 16, 129.
  *Ventilated,* 136, &c.

Hops,

# INDEX.

Hops, *their different Degrees of Heat in drying,* 141.
Horses, *in Ships to preserve,* 33.
Hospital-Ships, *to ventilate,* 83.
Hospitals, *to ventilate,* 23, 50.

### I.

Infants, *hurt by Swathing,* 77.
   *Their Skulls ought not to be compressed,* 78.
Infection, *enters by the Breath,* 40.
   *To cure by Fumigation,* 51, 52.

### L.

Larders, *to be ventilated,* 158.
Leakages, *to stop in Ships,* 67.

### M.

Magazines, *to ventilate,* 16, 20, 124.
Malt, *to ventilate,* 16.
   *Ventilators,* 129.
   *Kilns to order,* 138.
   *Dryed with cold Air,* 153.
   *With hot Air,* 155.
Mills, *will easily ventilate Corn,* 108.
   *Will winnow Corn,* 110.
Mines, *to ventilate,* 16, 17, 20.
   *Their several kinds of Damps,* 21.
Mows, *of Corn to dry,* 115.
Mustiness, *to cure,* 70.

## O.

Oak, *will not imbibe Oil*, 163.
Oil, *will not soak into Oak*, 163.

## P.

Pantreys, *to be ventilated*, 158.
Pease, *in Ships to preserve*, 60, 61, 62.
Pepper, *white, to ventilate*, 158.
Perspiration, *its Quantity*, 32, 42, 43.
   *Its Matter noxious*, 42.
Plague, *its Infection to cure*, 54.

## R.

Regulator, *described*, 5.
Respiration, *the Quantity carried off by it*, 43.
   *How affected by a dry Air*, 106.
Respirator, *its Description and Use*, 66.
Ricks, *of Corn, to dry*, 115.
Rivers, *why they freeze first at bottom*, 72.
   *Their upper Water descends towards the bottom*, 72.
Rooms, *close, the Inconveniencies of them*, 48.

## S.

Safes, *to be ventilated*, 158.
Sea-Water, *descends and ascends, at great Depths*, 73.
Ships, *to ventilate*, 24, &c.

# INDEX.

Ships, *Hospital, to ventilate*, 33.
 *New, unhealthy*, 33.
 *Preserved by Ventilation*, 34.
 *To be much ventilated*, 38.
 *To fumigate*, 51, to 54.
 *Their Leakages to stop*, 67, 68.
 *Worms to destroy*, 161.
 *Sheathing to make durable*, 164.
Smoke, *a Room cleared of it by Ventilation*, 16, 59.
Spirits, *distilled, their pernicious Effects*, 112, 160.
Swathing, *bad for Infants*, 76.

### T.

Tar, *Fumigation with it*, 52.

### U.

Valves, *described*, 9.
Ventilators, *large, their Description*, 3, &c.
 *To be moved by a Horse or Water*, 16, 17.
 *Double or treble*, 18.
 *Upright described*, 19.
 *Their Usefulness in Ships*, 38, to 49.
 *Small described*, 56.
 *Their Uses*, 59, &c. 65, 69.
 *For Corn*, 100, 151.
 *To be fixed in Mills*, 108.
 *Will carry off noxious Vapours*, 127.
 *Will dry and preserve Wool, Feathers*, 128.

# INDEX.

Ventilators, *will refresh in hot Climates,* 128.
  *For Hops and Malt,* 129, 131.
  *How to move with Horse or Mill,* 144, &c.
Ventilation, *its Labour in Ships, not great,* 35.
  *Its Importance,* 39, 41.
  *Its Use in cooling Beer,* 128.
Verdigrease, *to prevent Worms,* 165.
Vermine, *to destroy,* 55.
Vinegar, *its Use in Ships,* 45.
  *Its Use in sick Chambers,* 46.

## W.

Water, *stinking to sweeten,* 69, &c.
  *Putrid or stinking, will clean Bottles, and sweeten musty Casks,* 70.
Wells, *to ventilate,* 20.
  *Of Ships to ventilate,* 65.
  *To go with safety into them,* 67.
Wheat, *the Vacancy between its Grains,* 85.
  *One Tenth heavier than Water,* 85.
  *Washed and Kiln-dryed, not good,* 97.
  *Ventilated good,* 97.
  *Forty Bushels, are equal to fifty and a half Cubick Feet,* 108.
  *The Quantity of its Moisture when washed,* 109.
  *Cold, will soon be dryed,* 110.
Wind-sails, *their Defects,* 31, 38.
Work-Houses, *to ventilate,* 22, 50.
Worms, *of Ships, to prevent,* 161, *to* 165.

## THE END.

Fig: 4.

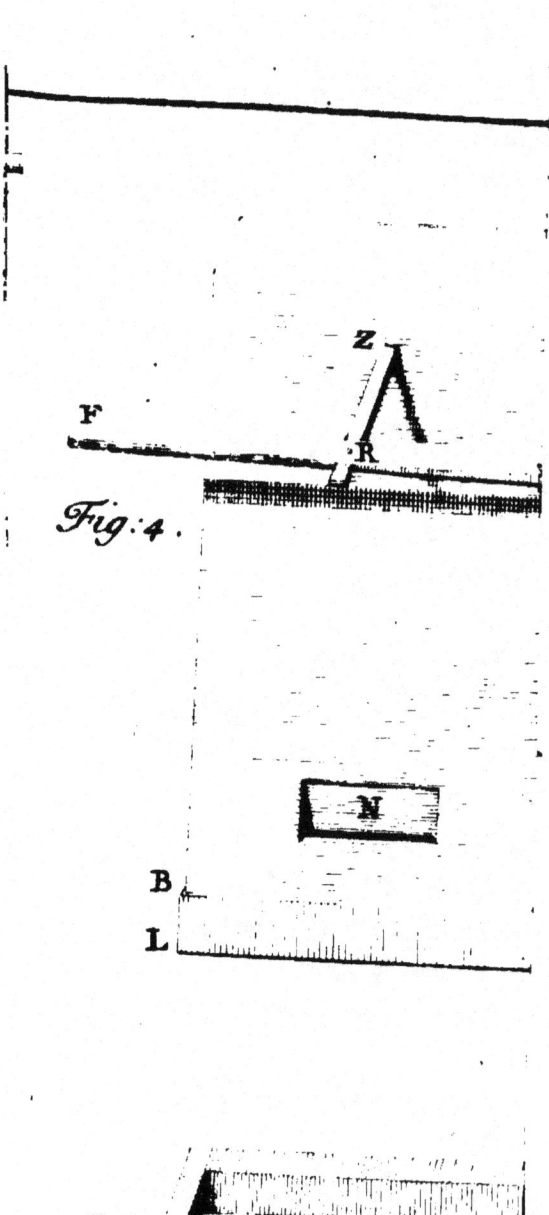

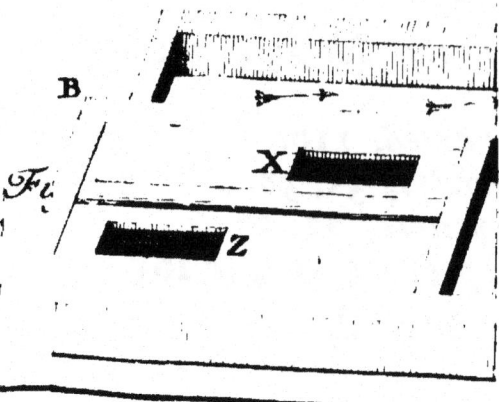

Fig: 11.

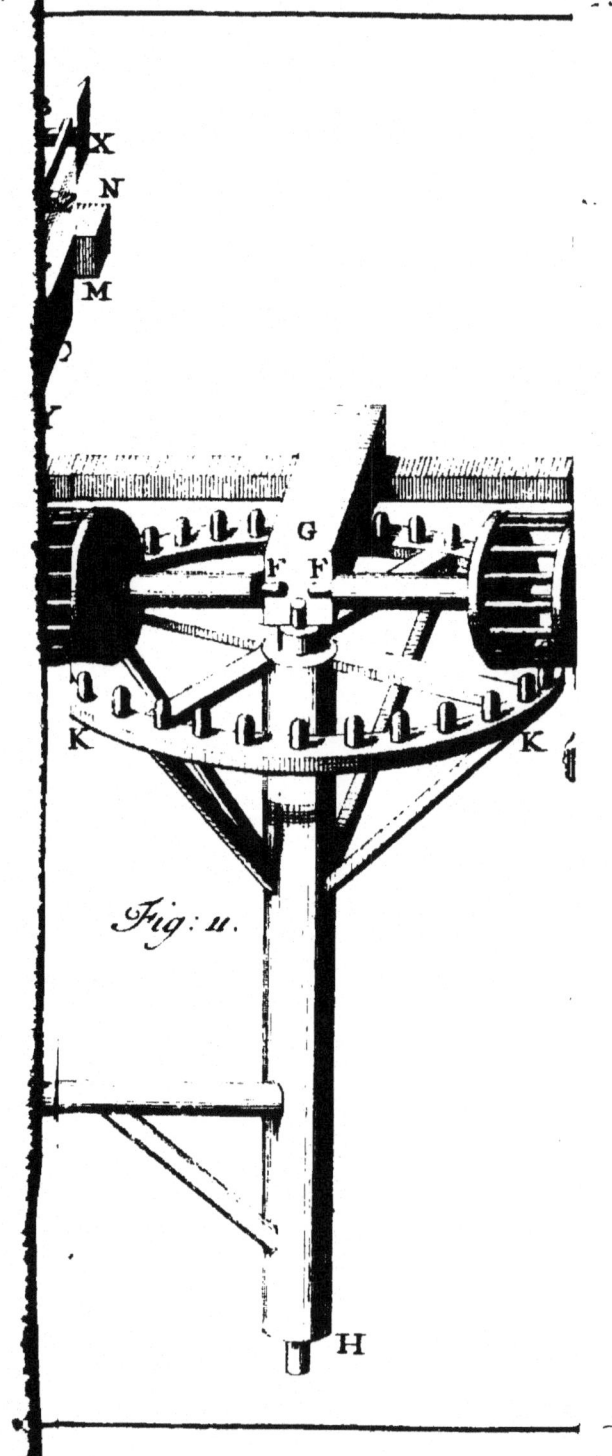